EAR TRAINING AND SIGHT-SINGING

D0127363

Ear Training and Sight-Singing

and

An Integrated Approach

BOOK 1

Allen R. Trubitt
Robert S. Hines

L.D.S.C. DISCARD LIBRARY

SCHIRMER BOOKS

A Division of Macmillan Publishing Co., Inc.

New York

Collier Macmillan Publishers

London

Copyright © 1979 by SCHIRMER BOOKS, A Division of Macmillan
Publishing Co., Inc.

All rights reserved. No part of this book may be reproduced or transmitted
in any form or by any means, electronic or mechanical, including
photocopying, recording, or by any information storage and retrieval
system, without permission in writing from the Publisher.

SCHIRMER BOOKS
A Division of Macmillan Publishing Co., Inc.
866 Third Avenue, New York, N.Y. 10022

Collier Macmillan Canada, Ltd.

Library of Congress Catalog Card Number: 77-5214

Printed in the United States of America

printing number
2 3 4 5 6 7 8 9 10

Library of Congress Cataloging in Publication Data

Trubitt, Allen R oy, 1931-
    Ear training and sight-singing.

    1. Ear training. 2. Sight-singing. I. Hines,
Robert St ephan 1926- joint author. II. Title.
MT35.T86 AP   784.9'4   77-5214
    ISBN 0-02-870810-5

We are grateful to Belwin Mills Publishing Corp., Melville, N.Y.,
Editions Salabert, Paris, Instituto de Investigaciones Esteticas, Mexico
City, Oxford University Press, London, G. Schirmer, Inc., New York,
and Universal Edition (London) Ltd., London, for permission to reprint
several melodies, as indicated in the text.

DESIGN BY SOHO STUDIO

To Germaine

CONTENTS

PREFACE

In the development of a musician no aspect of training is more crucial than the constant improvement of aural awareness. Accurate intonation, error detection, sight-reading—these and other activities are constantly required of the muscian, whose competence will in large part depend on his or her ability to hear music accurately and to relate what is heard to the notated music.

There is no shortage of texts that attempt to guide the developing musician toward greater aural competence. Perhaps the numerous workbooks and manuals attest to the difficulty in teaching this elusive subject. For, after all, hearing goes on in one's mind; the necessary gauging, comparing, and relating of tones is entirely a mental process, the details of which can only be known to the individual.

It is a fairly easy matter to test aural awareness, and many of the available texts depend heavily on this approach: the student is presented with a series of graded exercises, often with little or no advice about how to learn them. Success is claimed if the student improves. But the question remains as to whether anything was taught; did the text really help, or was it only a set of hurdles for the student to jump over. Recognizing that improving aural skills is an individual matter, we have tried to focus the student's attention in a way that will facilitate the learning process. The relative merits of texts and workbooks aside, the ultimate responsibility for improvement in aural awareness lies with the individual.

This text was written primarily for students who are planning a career in music. We have assumed that students will have a solid knowledge of music notation and elementary theory. Brief remarks about theoretical concepts are presented, but these are only by way of reminders. Students who are not familiar with scales, intervals, and simple chord construction must get that information from another source. Generally, we have assumed that this text will be used in an aural training course taught concurrently with a course in music theory.

Many of the exercises in this book require practice. Therefore, the student must be willing to budget sufficient daily practice time to make substantial progress. On page 313 will be found a progress chart which the student should fill out at the end of each practice or class session. If this seems too bothersome the chart should be reviewed when each unit has been completed. Filling out the progress chart will help the student keep track of the progress made, help identify persistent problems, and serve as a reminder that one is responsible for one's own development as a musician.

Some of the exercises included in this book are of a familiar type: sight-singing and dictation exercises are indispensable in developing aural awareness. We would like to make a special plea that the less familiar exercises not be omitted. Intonation, scanning, fusing, anticipation, and visual-recognition exercises provide an avenue for the individual to learn how his or her own ear functions most efficiently. We believe these new types of exercises represent the most important contribution this text may make in aural training.

Some of the exercises are quite difficult. This has been done intentionally, for two reasons. First, the text is intended for prospective professional musicians. We believe progress is hastened if one has a fuller picture of the difficulties involved—one should know what materials ultimately must be mastered. Second, every musician's ear can be improved, and this improvement should be a lifetime effort. Musicians at all levels should be able to find some exercises here that will offer challenges and opportunities for growth. In trying out the exercises, we have frequently found ourselves caught short on a passage which turned out to require more than casual attention. Any musician who can perform all the exercises in this text without a second glance has our admiration.

We have presented the material in the order and fashion which seemed best for the development of the concepts and skills herein. Sufficient variety has been provided to allow the teacher to direct the course as he or she chooses. Most teachers will find more material included than can be covered in the average one-year college course.

We have relied heavily on exercises that we have composed. The debate on the relative merits of using composed examples or examples from music literature will probably continue for years to come, along with the arguments about the pros and cons of the "movable" or "fixed *do*" solfeggio systems. We do not hope to resolve either of these perennial issues.

In most cases we have used terminology which is in general use, but we have not attempted to credit the authors or texts which first proposed some of the terms. Similarly, we hope the new terms we propose will prove useful enough to warrant general acceptance. In that happy event, future authors are free to adopt these terms without formal citation.

The recorded tapes that are such an integral part of this book may be purchased by schools adopting this text from Schirmer Books. The tapes, which may be copied, are intended to allow each student to work independently, practicing and reinforcing the various skills. A variety of instruments and voices have been used in the recordings to provide interest and a wide range of aural experiences.

We have observed that a good investment for the student is a reel-to-reel or cassette playback unit for home practice. Another piece of equipment every musician must have is a metronome. Many of the exercises in this book are to be performed at a specific tempo. In addition to establishing exact tempos, a metronome can be an invaluable aid in perfecting one's rhythmic awareness and rhythmic performance.

Many people at the University of Hawaii were extremely helpful in the development of this text. We are indebted to our colleagues LaVar Krantz, Neil McKay, Lewis Rowell, Floyd Uchima, and Byron Yasui for testing and discussing these texts, and to Barbara Smith for helping locate suitable ethnic materials. Special thanks to Armand Russell for reading the manuscript and offering encouragement and valuable suggestions which we often adopted. Mervin Britton and Margaret Goding also offered opinions and ideas that were helpful, even though they may have been altered beyond recognition. We are also indebted to Sinergia, Inc., for recording and editing the tapes. Finally, we would like to express our gratitude to those students who formed our "experimental classes" for the 1975–1978 academic years. Their intense interest, frankness, and time spent discussing and evaluating materials helped immeasurably in arriving at the final manuscript.

UNIT 1

PITCH

Matching Pitches Reference Pitch (RP)

A basic skill every musician must develop is the ability to *hear*, then *sing* a pitch that is sounded. This technique is called *matching pitches*.

Sound a tone on the piano or ask a friend to play or sing a single tone. This is the *reference pitch* (RP). Listen to the RP carefully, for an integral part of learning this skill is making absolutely sure that the RP is repeated exactly in tune, neither below (flat) nor above (sharp) the given pitch. Special effort must be made at the outset of ear training studies to achieve precise intonation, because, if careless intonation is not corrected early, a poor sense of pitch may persist throughout later stages of musical development. Remember, an out-of-tune pitch is a *wrong* note.

CONFERENCE: On Conferences

From time to time the authors would like to engage you in semi-private conferences about how to get the most from the various exercises in this book. These discussions will deal with your attitude, your way of seeing things, and your way of working with concepts.

Each musical exercise should be approached with all the care and prior consideration you would give to performing a significant masterwork for an audience. Exercises in this text are not purported to be great works of art. For the most part they have been designed to focus on specific problems of rhythm or pitch. However, to gain maximum benefit, the student is urged to view each exercise as an opportunity for *performance*.

Tape 1-1*___Matching Pitches

In this exercise you will hear a series of single tones. Listen carefully to each tone; when it stops, match the pitch by singing. Sustain the tone until you hear it once again on the tape. Compare your pitch with the tape for accuracy of intonation.

Instrumentalists and pianists can practice this exercise a second way: repeat the tones heard by playing them on your instrument instead of singing them. This may involve some searching at first, but eventually this exercise will develop the facility to transfer heard pitches into accurately fingered and played sounds—a skill worth having. However, this exercise should not be substituted entirely for matching pitches vocally.

CONFERENCE: Octave Displacement

When men and women sing together, or when a person tries to sing an instrumental melody, it often happens that the RP is beyond the person's vocal range. When this happens the singer will sing a tone which is higher or lower by one or more octaves. The RP is not being "matched" in a strict sense, but the octave or the double or triple octave are so similar to the unison that for all practical purposes we consider this to be the same pitch. Still, you should be aware that the RP may not really be in your range and that the pitch you are singing may be a large distance from the RP.

If you have any difficulty in matching a given pitch, begin at once to practice this skill until it is fully mastered. Your future progress as a musician depends upon it.

Tonal Memory

Matching pitches is the first requisite of musical aptitude. Because music extends over a span of time,

---

*If your tape playback unit has a counter, use this space to indicate the location of each exercise. This will make replaying exercises more convenient.

the second fundamental skill is *tonal memory*, the ability to remember a pitch or series of pitches.

Tape 1-2____Tonal Memory

You will hear three tones, followed by a pause. During the pause, sing the *first* tone (the reference pitch—RP) of the group. After the pause in which you have sung, the RP will be played again, so you can check your intonation. If the RP is not in your vocal range, sing it an octave higher or lower.

RHYTHM

Pulse, Basic Duration, and Count

In dealing with rhythm, one of the most commonly used terms is *beat*. It is not used only to refer to the regular accents which form the temporal framework of most of our music. Beat is such a general term that it is useful to separate some of its meanings. Consider these common phrases: "Play on the beat"; "hold that note for two beats"; "we will beat this in four." To separate these concepts we will use *pulse* to refer to the regular accents which mark off the time units. The time elapsing between pulses will be called *basic duration* (BD).

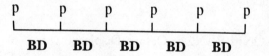

In rehearsing, musicians often use a metronome, count aloud, tap something, or snap their fingers: these are audible ways of indicating the beginning of each time unit. These short sounds indicate the pulses. Note that pulse is only an instant, it has no apparent duration. The time elapsing between the pulses, determines the *tempo*. If the BD is very short, the tempo is fast. For musical purposes the maximum speed is about two hunded pulses per minute. (If you set your metronome to that speed you will see that it would be difficult to count pulses at that speed for very long.) If the BD is long, the tempo is slow. The minimum practical speed is about thirty pulses per minute (M.M. = 30).

When we speak of "beating this in four" we are referring to the conductor's beat or to the performer's own counting. Most often, the *count* will be the same as the audible pulse or "beat" of the music. However, there are times when, for accuracy, security, or comfort, a performer may choose to count more or fewer pulses than the audible beat. We will pursue this concept in greater detail later; for now, you should be aware that how you count a piece of music will have a great effect on your performance.

Exercise 1-1   Basic Duration

a. Set the metronome at 76 pulses per minute, then snap your fingers or tap along with the pulses. As you do so, pay particular attention to precision. The clicks of the metronome and your tapping should coincide exactly. Concentrate on the pulses.

b. As you continue to tap, shift your attention to the *basic duration,* that is, notice the time elapsing, rather than focusing on the pulses.

c. Set the metronome faster, to 120. Then to 184. Perform a. and b. at these faster tempos.

d. Review the meanings of foreign words used to indicate various tempos (tempi) in a good dictionary of musical terms.

Tones and Rests of One Basic Duration

In musical notation, the basic duration (BD) may be represented by any note value (𝅝 , 𝅗𝅥 , 𝅘𝅥 , 𝅘𝅥𝅮). In practice, however, three values have been used most frequently; the half note 𝅗𝅥 , the quarter note 𝅘𝅥 , and the eighth note 𝅘𝅥𝅮 .* It is assumed that the student is familiar with these symbols and the corresponding rests which are used for *silent periods* equal in length to the notes.

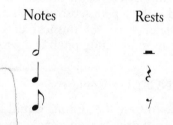

| Notes | Rests |

Notice that these symbols represent durations, time elapsing. They do not indicate pulses.

A musical tone has three elements: *attack*, or beginning; *duration*; and *release*. In the following exercises, assume that each 𝅘𝅥 or 𝄽 represents one basic duration.

Exercise 1-2   Intoning Rhythm

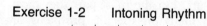

Intone: ta ta ta ta ta
Be sure that each "ta" extends from one pulse to the next.

*This applies to simple meters; compound meters will be discussed later.

Tap: ♩ ♩ ♩ ♩ ♩ ♩

Note that the duration of the taps is so short that the effect is of an instantaneous sound, one not having duration. When tapping, clapping, counting, or otherwise marking time, always be aware that you are merely marking the pulses, not actually sustaining the sound throughout the BD. Percussionists must be especially aware of this fact.

An extended succession of undifferentiated pulses is rather rare in music. Usually, a pattern of accent emerges.* This pattern may be perceived through regular emphasis in dynamics

♩ ♩ ♩ ♩ ♩ ♩ ♩ ♩ ♩

or the accent may simply be implied or felt, even when no special effort is made to emphasize certain pulses.

♩ ♩ ♪ ♩ ♩ ♪ ♩ ♩ ♪

The pattern of accent used in a musical composition is called meter and is indicated by a *meter signature* at the beginning of a work. Students using this text should be familiar with the traditional signatures. In addition to the standard meter signatures we shall use a modified type, employed by some twentieth-century composers, which avoids some of the confusion that tends to develop about meter. In this modified meter signature, the upper *number* indicates the number of pulses in a measure. The lower note ($\frac{4}{♩} = \frac{4}{4}$, $\frac{3}{\rho} = \frac{3}{2}$) indicates the value representing the basic duration.

Students should also be aware of the significance of the barline and the implied accent which it denotes.

Exercise 1-3　Rehearsed Rhythm: Two or More BDs

Set the metronome at the speed indicated and intone the pattern. Be sure to sustain all tones up to the following pulse.

*Further discussion of accents will be found in Unit 6.

♩ = 132

e. [musical notation in 3/2 time]

♪ = 120

f. [musical notation in 3/8 time]

It should be clear when comparing e. and f., the last two exercises, that relative note values are in force only when the values appear in the same work. Taken separately, half notes are not necessarily longer than eighths.

Note: the whole rest may be used to indicate a complete measure of silence regardless of the meter (see a. above).

Tones and Rests of Two or More Basic Durations

Thus far we have limited ourselves to tones and rests of one *basic duration*. A tone may, of course, extend beyond one BD.

[musical notation example]

The ties in the above example indicate that the release and attack which otherwise would separate these notes have been omitted. The result is a longer tone, two or more BDs in length. When intoning a rhythm involving a tied note, sustain the tone evenly and do not emphasize or attack the pulse of the tied note.

Exercise 1-4   Rehearsed Rhythm

Notice that each of the above exercises ends with a tone, not a rest. In order to sustain the final tone for the full length of the BD, one must actually count or feel the pulse which would have come at the beginning of the next measure. Thus, to sustain a tone for four BDs one must hear *five* clicks of the metronome.

4

Note Values

In Exercise 1-4 a. and b. we saw how tones and rests may be added—joined together to produce longer values. The relative lengths may be represented by numbers.

From Exercise 1-4 a.

From Exercise 1-4 b.

Students are no doubt familiar with this chart of note values. Notice the ratio of 2:1.

By the use of dotted notes the ratio of 3:1 may be indicated.

The 3:1 ratio is often explained by this rule: A dot following a note increases the length of that note by half. (Double-dotted notes are less common, but the same rule applies: the second dot lengthens the first dot by half.)

A chart of all the common note values would appear:

Exercise 1-5   Note Values: Rhythm

In each of the following exercises locate the shortest note value. Assume that it has a value of one BD. Indicate what the relative values of the other notes would be (see Exercise 1-5 a.). If notes are tied or rests follow rests, indicate the total length of the combined tones or rests.

In notating a piece of music, composers select a convenient note value to represent the basic duration. There are some traditions involved in the choice but, theoretically, any value may be chosen. Once the choice is made the table of relative values applies.

Exercise 1-6   Note Values

Write these rhythms without any meter signature or barlines.

If the BD is
represented by: the rhythm is:

a. ♩   1 1 2 1 1 3 1 2 2 4

b. ♪   3 2 1 2 3 4 6 1 1 2

c. ♩   5 3 2 1 4 6 1 2 4 5

d. ♩   2 3 1 4 3 2 4 1 1 2

e. ♩.   1 1 2 2 4 3 1

f. ♩♪   2 4 3 5 1 3 2 4

g. ♬   2 8 6 4 2 1 5 4

h. ♩   4 3 7 2 1 5 4 1

The standard for correct notation is set by usage. Changes develop over a period of time as in language, but certain principles are firmly established and should always be observed. As long as whole BDs are used, the familiar notes and rests easily indicate the required rhythm.

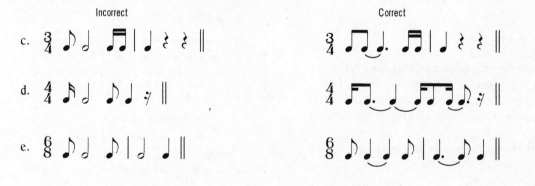

When notes and rests are used to represent durations smaller than one BD the rhythm must be written so each divided BD is visually complete. In the following incorrectly notated examples some notes overlap (their value is divided between two BDs) in a way that requires cumbersome calculation; one cannot *see* each complete BD.

6

Exercise 1-7   Rhythm

Rewrite Exercise 1-4, replacing tied notes by larger note values wherever possible. A tie across a barline cannot be replaced by longer note values. Why? If you have some experience in reading music, compare the relative ease of reading your rewritten version with Exercise 1-4.

CONFERENCE: Practice with a Partner

If you seriously wish to make rapid progress in aural training, we suggest you find a person in your class who is willing to practice with you. (From experience we have observed that students who pair up with a "buddy" invariably do better work.) Schedule regular meeting times; otherwise it becomes too easy to find reasons to postpone sessions.

During practice sessions you will soon learn one another's strong and weak points; concentrate on those areas that are problematic. The opportunity to exchange thoughts on what makes a listening experience easy or difficult may bring out solutions not mentioned in class or in this book. Students learn from one another, so talk about techniques of aural training with classmates and other music students.

UNIT 2

RHYTHM

Counting

Musicians often have difficulty with rhythms because they are not sufficiently aware of how their counting may affect performance. Counting means more than simply keeping track of the meter. Once the pulse has been established the performer has the responsibility of producing tones in accurate coordination with the pulse. In some simple pieces all of the tones are one or more full BDs in length. In these cases each tone begins and ends on a particular pulse. More often the music requires the performer to produce some tones which are shorter than one BD, that is, to "divide time." To describe the divisions the performer must make we will use the term "rhythmic level." If the BD is divided in halves, this is called "rhythmic level 2." If it is divided in thirds, it is called "level 3"; in fourths, "level 4," and so on.

The choice of rhythmic level is left to the performer. The composer has indicated a meter signature, but this refers to how *he* thinks the rhythm should be heard. What goes on in the performer's mind is his own business! Thus, the listener may perceive a work moving at a speed of ♩ = 72, while the performer may actually be counting ♪ = 144. Especially in practicing, the choice of level can be critical in obtaining rhythmic accuracy in the most efficient way.

As mentioned above, there are songs and other short pieces that involve only Level 1 rhythms, i.e., no tones or rests *shorter* than one BD in length. Beginning method books for piano and other instruments often remain at Level 1 for a long time; the rhythmic problems are thus kept at a minimum so the student's attention can focus on other technical problems.

Au claire de la lune

Twinkle, Twinkle, Little Star

All of the exercises in Unit 1 were at rhythmic Level 1. Let us now consider tones and rests shorter than one BD.

Long, Long Ago

Throughout this melody the BD is frequently divided into two eighths. This is Level 2: rhythms that *divide* the BD in halves. Perform the following experiment: sing through "Long, Long Ago" while tapping your foot to every quarter. Now sing through the song again, tapping every eighth. Theoretically, there may be no difference in how the melody sounds, but there certainly is a difference in how it feels to change the rhythmic level. If the song is performed tapping quarters, the flow of the melody is much smoother; the quarters simply *divide* into two eighths where necessary. This is Level 2. On the other hand, singing the melody while tapping the eighths feels quite different: the melody does not flow as well, but there is greater control over the rhythm, a sense of greater accuracy. There is no need to *divide*, for each ♪ receives a pulse; we are at Level 1.*

Throughout the remainder of this book we will be considering smaller and smaller divisions, down to Level 8. You should always remember that you have the option of shifting the pulse. Remember: greater accuracy will be obtained at the rhythmic level requiring the fewest divisions, while greater flow will be apparent at higher levels. Thus, if a passage involving thirty-second notes presents a problem when a pulse is felt on each quarter, there is the option of feeling a pulse on each ♪ (Level 1) or on each ♪ (Level 2). Once accuracy is attained, the pulse can be felt on each ♪ (Level 4) or each ♩ (Level 8). The effect of shifting levels is similar to using lenses of varying power on a microscope.

Tape 2-1____Listening: Rhythm

You will hear a folksong played with a metronome marking the pulses. The first time, the metronome will indicate pulses at Level 1 (the level of the shortest note values). The second time the metronome will mark pulses at Level 2.

Notice that, counting at Level 1, the performer need not "divide." Greater accuracy is attained, although the musical effect is somewhat pedestrian, considering the context.

Remember that the rhythmic level is chosen by the performer to suit the musical needs at any given time.

Level 2 Rhythm (Simple Division)

The number of possible rhythms at Level 2 is not great, but it is essential that these rhythms be learned with complete accuracy before going on to other levels.

Let us see first how these rhythms appear with various note values representing the BD. Notice that if the ♩ or ♪ represents the BD the beaming may be useful in quickly identifying the groups (♩ = ♫, ♪ = ♬).

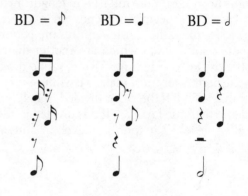

BD = ♪   BD = ♩   BD = ♩

Exercise 2-1   Imitation: Rhythm—Level 1 and Level 2

Your teacher or a fellow student will tap, clap, or intone one measure of Level 1 and Level 2 rhythms. At a signal, imitate what you have heard. The metronome should be set at 92 throughout this exercise.

* Level 1 is the level of the shortest note value. The concept of level may be equated with division, i.e., if one divides each BD into halves, one is at Level 2. If one divides each pulse into four, one is at Level 4.

Exercise 2-2   Rehearsed Rhythm

With the metronome set at ♩ = 92, intone these rhythms.

a. (musical notation in 4/4)

b. (musical notation in 4/4)

c. (musical notation in 4/4)

With the pulse at ♪ = 92, which measures employ only Level 1 rhythms? What must be done to perform the remaining measures at Level 1? (Answer on page **264**.)

Tape 2-2 — Anticipation: Rhythm

On this tape you will hear each bar of Exercise 2-2 played, separated by one measure of silence. During the silence, try to anticipate, to "hear" the following measure. Immediately afterward the tape will play the rhythms correctly. Thus you can practice your ability to "hear" silently. This is very important work; do not omit this opportunity to develop your "inner ear."

Exercise 2-3   Rehearsed Rhythm: Dotted Rhythms

The following exercise should be practiced until there is no hesitation in performance. For accuracy, each exercise may also be practiced with a pulse for each of the shortest note values, i.e., at Level 1.

f. ♩ = 96

The rhythm ♩ ♫ ♩ is also a Level 2 rhythm, since the shortest note value (♪) has a ratio of 2:1 to the count (♩). This rhythm is often written ♩. ♪, which must be learned so that this common figure is quickly identified.

In learning this rhythm or in trying to solve some particular problem involving it, it might be best to work at Level 1, with a pulse on each ♪. At this level a student cannot escape the 3:1 ratio of the note values.

♩ = 112

Suppose a performer has the following rhythm to execute:

It would probably be a waste of energy to perform this entire exercise counting eighths. The performer may change the pulse in midstream, say at the beginning of the fourth measure of the following.

Pulse

Using this approach the performer would anticipate the ♩. ♪ figure and shift to a pulse on each ♪ sufficiently in advance so that there is no interruption in his counting or performance.

Exercise 2-4   Rehearsed Rhythm

Throughout this book, rhythmic exercises should be practiced and performed as "duets" with a metronome. Tempo indications should be strictly observed.

The following exercises should be performed so that a pulse is felt on each shortest note value (counted at Level 1). When Level 2 rhythm is approaching, shift the pulse accordingly not less than two BDs earlier.

Level 1 (♪)   Level 2 (♫)

When the above rhythms are mastered at Level 1, repeat them at Level 2.

Tape 2-3____Error Correction: Rhythm

If the rhythms heard on the tape are correctly notated below, do nothing. If wrong, write an X over that measure.

Syncopation and Upbeats

Another Level 2 rhythm which needs particular attention is $\frac{4}{4}$ ♪♩ ♩ ♩ ♪♩ .

This common syncopation often gives a great deal of trouble. It should be practiced first as a Level 1 rhythm, beginning with a comfortable slow tempo and gradually becoming faster until the figure can be performed at Level 2 without dislocating the syncopation. Eventually the student should be able to sustain this rhythm comfortably at M.M. = 120.

One final point remains to be made about Level 2 rhythms. Sometimes a piece begins with an upbeat in the middle of the BD. When this happens, the performer should feel the pulse of the full BD before starting. This example

should be performed with the pulse as shown.

Pulse (♩)

Exercise 2-5   Rehearsed Rhythm

a.

b.

From what American folksong is this last rhythmic example taken? (See Unit 2 answers.)

Exercise 2-6   Rehearsed Rhythm

Intone while tapping the BD. Most of the exercises should be performed entirely at Level 2, but a shift to Level 1 may be helpful in a difficult passage.

a.

b.

c.

d.

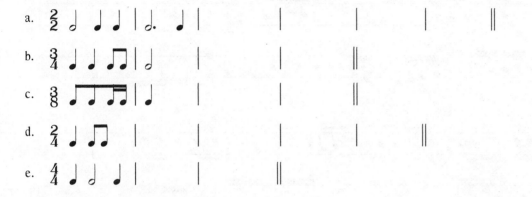

♩ = 112   More Difficult

e.

♪ = 88

f.

Tape 2-4___Dictation: Rhythm

Complete the notation in the following examples.

a.

b.

c.

d.

e.

SIGHT-READING

♩ = 80

1

♩ = 112   Tricky!

2

♩ = 96

3

♪ = 104

4

CONFERENCE: Scanning

Improving your ability to sight-read depends a great deal on your attitude. As in learning to read words, it is important to keep your eyes moving, to force yourself, if necessary, to look ahead. Once you have gotten your eyes to look ahead, you must develop confidence that you (can) remember what you saw. Try not to look back.

Scanning exercises will help you to train your eyes to see ahead. They will also give you a taste of improvisation, since you must determine the pitches to be sung. All that is shown is the general contour of

the melody. Assume that the two *horizontal* lines are the top and bottom lines of the musical staff. You are to follow the rise and fall of the tones as indicated, but the exact pitches are up to you. As you approach the cadence at the end of a phrase, try to find pitches which will bring the phrase to a satisfactory conclusion. If you cannot always do this, do not be discouraged; improvisation is also a skill which will develop with practice. In any case, *do not stop:* the basic purpose of the scanning exercises is to gain fluency. Choose a neutral syllable (la, ta, lu) and plunge in.

15

CONFERENCE: Reference Pitches

One's ability to perform music, and in fact one's ability to understand it, depends to a large degree on tonal memory—the ability to recall a particular pitch. It is very difficult to define or describe the feeling of tonal center or "tonic," but every musician understands the concept. You may have learned to sight-sing using the traditional solfeggio syllables, do–re–mi–fa–sol–la–ti–do. The purpose of this system is to reinforce tonal memory.

Whether you use this system or not, you must constantly work to improve your tonal memory. A pitch that is kept in the memory is called a *reference pitch* (RP). The most important RP will almost always be the tonic pitch. However, as you gain experience in sight-singing, you will discover the importance of retaining several tones in your memory.

Throughout the exercises in this book you will come across tones which are suggested as RPs. They will be indicated thus:

When you begin to practice or perform a melody, establish the RP clearly in mind. If you aren't sure, don't go on.

As you continue through the melody, other tones may attract your attention, either because of their frequent use, prominent position, or special relationship to other tones. If such a tone begins to stick in your memory, it may become an additional RP. The more RPs you can retain, the better.

There are two ways to find pitches in the course of a melody, an *absolute approach* and a *relative approach*. Using the absolute approach, you recall the pitch from your memory bank, where it was "stored" as an RP. Using the relative approach, you locate the new pitch by its distance or relationship from a known pitch, i.e., another RP. The ability to retain an RP is basic. Without it, one's ability to function musically will be severely limited.

INTERVALS

An interval is the distance between two tones. If the two tones are sounded in succession the result is a *melodic interval*; if they are sounded simultaneously a *harmonic interval* results.

Seconds—Major and Minor

Our study of intervals begins with the *seconds*, major and minor. These intervals form the basis of most of the scales used in Western music. They have been called the building blocks of melody.

The minor second, m2, is formed when two tones are one half step (semitone) apart.

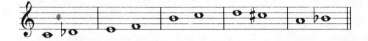

Notice that in each of the above intervals *two degrees* are involved (C and D, E and F, etc.). A less common interval is the *chromatic semitone*, which also has one half step between the tones, but involves chromatic alteration of the same scale degree.

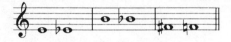

The *major second*, M2, is formed when two tones are two half steps, one whole tone, apart.

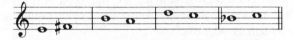

CONFERENCE: Singing Seconds

In singing seconds melodically, the feeling is usually one of going to the *next* tone up or down in the scale. If the scale is familiar you may not even have to think about whether you are singing m2 or M2. But in unfamiliar scales you must be able to sing M2 or m2 as required.

CONFERENCE: Hearing and Singing Intervals

Aural experiences take precedence over theoretical discussions in this textbook. If a section of a unit occasionally moves into the realm of music theory, the purpose will be to help you hear, understand, and perform better that which appears in the score.

There are some basic facts regarding the hearing and singing of intervals that you must keep in mind:

1. *Every interval is a unique aural experience.* Concentrate on and memorize its special qualities when sounded, either melodically or harmonically.

2. *Melodic interval.* The *distance* between successively sounded pitches is generally more evident because of the movement, up or down, than when the same interval is sounded harmonically.

3. *Harmonic interval.* The *sonority* of simultaneously sounding pitches results in a specific aural experience. Although describing the composite sound is difficult, the spacing of the sounding tones creates a unique *sonority*.

4. *Register and timbre.* Two factors that have a great deal to do with aural recognition are *register*—how high or low an interval is sounded, and *timbre*—the quality of the voices singing or the instruments playing an interval. The tapes prepared for this textbook were recorded with various instruments and voices to give you a variety of aural experiences.

Tape 2-5____Listening: Seconds

The intervals on this tape will be heard in this order:
  a. five major seconds, played melodically
     five major seconds, played harmonically
  b. five minor seconds, played melodically
     five minor seconds, played harmonically
  c. comparison of major second and minor second, played melodically (three sets)
  d. comparison of major second and minor second, played harmonically (three sets)

CONFERENCE: Sonority of M2 and m2

When listening to Tape 2-5 you should have noted the difference in *sonority* between the M2 and m2. While neither interval is consonant ("harmonious"), there is considerable difference in the *degree* of dissonance ("harshness"); the m2 is quite biting.

Exercise 2-8   Visual Recognition: Seconds

Visual recognition of intervals is a skill that must be developed. In reading music, visual recognition precedes aural responses and performance.

Do not look ahead at the exercise until you have read the instructions that follow.

1. Set your metronome at 60.

Take a piece of paper or a 3 × 5 card. Cover the first few measures. Slide the paper or card to the right, exposing measure one. Identify the interval shown within the timespan of four pulses. Move to the next interval still allowing only four pulses to identify the correct interval.

2. Note that the first fourteen exercises involve accidentals that appear within the measure while the second fourteen exercises have key signatures.

Now, if everything is ready, turn the book around and begin.

Tape 2-6____Tonal Memory

In this exercise you will hear four tones played successively, followed by a pause. During the pause, sing the four tones. The tape will then repeat the tones so you can check yourself.

Tape 2-7____Imitation with Notation: Seconds

A series of melodic major and minor seconds will be heard. Let your inner ear distinguish the difference in the *distance* between the M2 and m2. Sing along with the tape when it repeats the intervals, paying particular attention to your intonation.

CONFERENCE: Intonation

Learning to hear when a pitch or interval is exactly in tune is a skill which can hardly be taught; it is in the nature of a basic experience or skill that almost everyone possesses to some degree.

The exercise below is the first of a series emphasizing intonation. These exercises are extremely important for all musicians, regardless of their performing medium.

Your particular task is to adjust the intonation of each tone in relation to the RPs played as drones. Practice them this way:

1. Perform the exercises as slowly as possible. The tones in each bar are to be sung in one breath.

2. Black notes are to be sung short, white notes long.

3. Drones should be played so that the pitches being sung can be easily related to them. The guitar is ideal for playing the drone, but other instruments may be used.

4. If a pitch sounds out of tune, adjust the intonation, *then repeat the entire measure.* This is to adjust the melodic interval as well as the harmonic.

5. As you sustain each long pitch, be aware of the *sonority* of the interval formed by the drone and the sung note. Then, as you move to the next pitch, be aware of the *distance.* Try to develop your perception of the horizontal (distance) and the vertical (sonority) quality of each interval.

6. Since these exercises are to be sung as slowly as possible, it is important that your attention be carefully focused. Before beginning, it may be necessary to prepare yourself mentally. Adopt an attitude of quiet, patient attention. Do the best you can, but do not be frustrated if you discover that some of the pitches need repeated adjusting. You may actually get the impression for a while that you are getting worse. This is a common illusion; what may be really happening is that your ear is becoming sharper and you are becoming more aware of slight deviations in your intonation.

Exercise 2-9   Intonation: Seconds

Tape 2-8____Anticipation: Seconds

A measure of three pulses will be counted. Then you will hear the RP (note with stem down). In the silent bar that follows sing the next note. In the third measure you will hear the tone you should have sung.

Repeat the exercise until you can sing it without errors.

Major Seconds

Minor Seconds

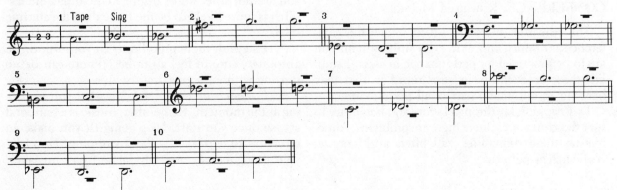

This exercise is designed to develop your ability to distinguish between the sonority of the major and minor second. Write *M* or *m* after each number.

Melodic

1 2 3 4 5 6 7 8 9 10

Harmonic

1 2 3 4 5 6 7 8 9 10

CONFERENCE: Composing Interval Drills

If you have difficulty identifying the major and minor second try inventing *interval drills* to practice while walking. You might try singing these:

1. Start low and ascend using this scale pattern:
   M2, m2, M2, m2, etc.
   M2, M2, m2, M2, M2, etc.
2. Start high and descend with this pattern:
   m2, M2, m2, M2, etc.
   m2, m2, M2, m2, m2, M2, etc.

Tape 2-10_____Error Correction: Intervals

One of the most important skills a musician must learn is the capacity to relate what he *sees* to what he *hears.* In this set, circle the number if the sounded interval is *not* the same as the written pitches. Assume that the first (or lower) pitch is always correct.

Examples 1 through 6 are melodic intervals, 7 through 12 harmonic.

Listen to this exercise again and write in or cross out accidentals where necessary so the notation indicates what is on the tape.

CONFERENCE: Rehearsed Melodies

The rehearsed melodies which follow this conference and which appear in every unit from now on are to be practiced for performance in class. Establish these rules firmly in your mind so that they become an automatic part of all performances.

1. Read quickly through before you begin; try to spot those measures where there are problems. Anticipating these difficulties will often avoid errors. Notice clear patterns.

Because repetition is so common in music there will often be only three or four basic rhythmic and melodic ideas in a short composition.

2. *Identify the principal RP* clearly in your ear. If you are not sure, don't begin! Remember, the last pitch is more likely to be the tonic than the starting pitch.

3. Establish the tempo firmly in your mind. Be absolutely sure to feel an upbeat; there can be no starting without a preparatory pulse.

4. *Concentrate* completely on what you are doing at the moment. Remember, music is a temporal art, so once you start, keep going. If you make an error, try to correct it without stopping. Don't let your thoughts move back to lament past mistakes.

5. ***Don't mix practicing and performing.*** But it is necessary to do both during rehearsal time. Practice first, carefully stopping to correct every error. You may have to stop and start many times over a two- or three-note figure. If a particular note seems to give you trouble, be sure to go back *before* that note; the problem is not the note itself, but getting into the note. *Pitches* are not usually difficult, but *intervals* often are.

6. When you have practiced a passage suffi-ciently, perform it. Adopt the mental set of a performer: concentrate, then play or sing through to the end of the passage without stopping or hesitating to correct any errors or problems that arise. Afterward make a critical review of the performance; you may discover areas where more practice is needed. If you are satisfied, go on to the next section.

To summarize: when practicing, stop for *everything* that goes wrong; when performing, stop for *nothing*.

REHEARSED MELODIES

SIGHT-READING

The following melodies are to be read at sight, *not* prepared.

For interesting variations, try singing these melodies with key signatures or clefs altered.

Carl Orff, *Carmina Burana* Reprinted by permission of Belwin Mills Publishing Corp., Melville, N.Y.

MORE DIFFICULT

(For the eager and ambitious)

CONFERENCE: Dictation

A good deal of mystique has become attached to the matter of writing down music. This activity is most used by composers, of course, but any musician who can read music should be able to write it. There are two aspects of dictation: familiarity with notation and tonal memory.

Your familiarity with notation is a reflection of your overall background in music theory and sight reading. Tonal memory is a skill which almost everyone has to some degree. There are exercises in memory throughout this book, but in fact the most difficult part of taking dictation is allowing one's ear to do its job. Often students become so concerned with writing down everything at once that they get in their own way. Here are some simple steps to follow in taking dictation:

1. Just listen to the music at first; do not try to write at all.

2. When you are fairly sure you have heard the music and have it in your inner ear, try to sing through it while tapping the pulses. Determine the meter and what kind of note will represent the BD. *Then try to visualize the rhythm of the music in notation.*

3. Now sing the music to yourself once again, locating the tonic and other RPs which become clear to you. At this point your knowledge of intervals will make all the difference. If you are quick to identify the various intervals, you will have little trouble with dictation.

The development of skill at dictation is like that of any other musical skill: practice makes perfect. If the only time you ever try to notate a melody is in class, you will probably not become very proficient. In practicing dictation it is not necessary to have someone play unfamiliar melodies for you; choose any melody, popular or classical, that you have heard but not seen notated, and try to write it down. The decisions you will have to make will be the same as with an unfamiliar piece. Remember to listen carefully until you are sure you have *heard* the music; don't be too eager to start writing.

Finally, a word about the way we memorize. If you are listening to a long melody you will probably hear the beginning and recall it. As the melody progresses you may not be able to follow it completely, and you may get lost in the middle. But when the melody ends, the closing tones will stick in your memory without effort. Make use of this fact. If you don't recall the middle for the moment, skip it and write the ending.

DICTATION

Tape 2-11____Intervals

Write the second note in each measure. Each interval will be played melodically once.

A.

For additional practice in dictation replay Tape 2-6 (Tonal Memory). Notate these motives. Starting notes are given below.

B.

UNIT 3

INTERVALS

Thirds—Major and Minor

The importance of the *major* and *minor thirds* (M3, m3) cannot be stressed too much. Along with the M2 and m2, thirds are essential structural materials in most of the folk music and composed melodies in music literature.

Likewise, thirds are vital to harmony: they imply major or minor mode, and they form the basis of tertian harmony—triads, seventh, ninth, eleventh and thirteenth chords.*

In singing thirds, one has the feeling of "skipping" a tone, as in the familiar broken-third sequence.

As with seconds, one does not have to think about whether a particular third is major or minor in the above pattern, so familiar is the major scale. But in less common circumstances you must be able to distinguish clearly the M3 from the m3.

*Ninth, eleventh, and thirteenth chords will be discussed in Book 2.

Harmonically, the thirds are highly preferred intervals. In many folksongs a second part may be added in parallel thirds throughout. The aural effect of the third is consonant, "harmonious."

Notice that the M3 is a brighter sonority than the m3.

Tape 3-1____Listening: Thirds

The M3 and m3 intervals will be played in this order:
   a. five major thirds, played melodically
      five major thirds, played harmonically
   b. five minor thirds, played melodically
      five minor thirds, played harmonically
   c. comparison of major and minor thirds, played melodically (three sets)
   d. comparison of major and minor thirds, played harmonically (three sets)

As you listen to the melodic intervals be aware of the *distance* between tones. As you listen to the harmonic intervals be aware of the *sonority*.

Exercise 3-1   Visual Recognition of Intervals

Set your metronome at 60. Allow three pulses to identify each interval. On the fourth pulse move the card one measure to the right and identify the next interval.

If 60 seems pedestrian try 92, 120, or 144.

Exercise 3-2   Intonation: Thirds

If you do not recall how these exercises should be performed, refer back to the intonation exercise in Unit 2 (page **18**).

1.   Major Third

2. Minor Third

3. Drone

Tape 3-2 _____ Tonal Memory

You will hear a series of five-tone exercises. After the five tones have been sounded there will be a pause during which you sing the tones; the example will be repeated so you can check your accuracy.

Tape 3-3 _____ Imitation with Notation: Thirds

The tape will play major and minor thirds. Listen to the interval while watching the music. In the following measure sing back what you heard. The music will indicate how the harmonic intervals are to be imitated.

CONFERENCE: Fusing

One of the basic skills in score reading is the ability to "hear" or imagine music from what is seen on the page. This skill is not easily acquired—not everyone can look at an orchestral score and hear every sound. But all musicians have to be able to do this to some extent.

The following exercise is called "fusing" and is designed to develop your skill in hearing harmonies.

It allows you to hear one pitch, imagine another, then hear both sounding simultaneously. There is no way to be graded by a teacher on this exercise since the work is done in your mind, but the mental practice will bring significant rewards if you are diligent.

Before you begin be sure you understand how the exercise is to be performed; otherwise it will seem pointless.

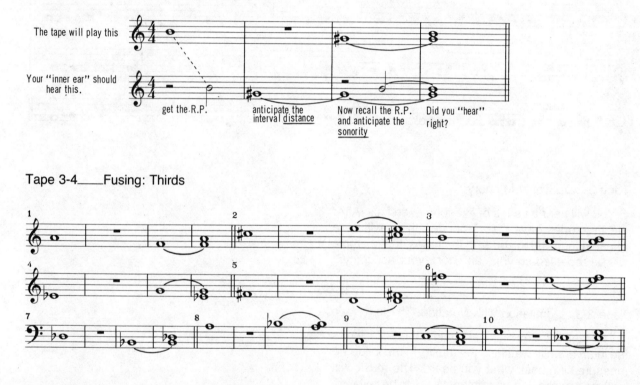

CONFERENCE: Learning Intervals

In the early stages of writing and singing intervals some students "build" them by half and whole steps. For example, to sing a major third, M3, they sing two major seconds from the RP. Similarly, some students use the device of a "reference melody." This is a familiar melody which has the particular interval in a prominent position, usually at the beginning. While these two methods may

work for a while, they add extra steps to the process of hearing and identifying the intervals. They are crutches which may not be discarded as quickly as they should. Therefore, while it may be harder to learn the intervals abstractly, without any reference to anything but the tones involved, it is preferable in the long run. Consider all intervals as basic phenomena and learn them as you would memorize vocabulary in a new language.

Tape 3-5____Anticipation: Thirds

The tape will play an RP in the first measure. In measure two, sing the notes given. The tape will repeat measure two so you can check your accuracy.

Tape 3-6____Aural Recognition: Thirds

The M3 and m3 will be heard on this tape. Mark M3 or m3 after each number.

1	2	3	4	5
6	7	8	9	10

Tape 3-7____Error Correction: Melody

An important part of a musician's craft is the ability to identify errors in performance from what is seen on the printed score.

Study this melody as you would one of the rehearsed melodies. *Do not play it on an instrument; develop and trust your inner hearing.*

When you are confident as to how it should sound, play the tape and circle places where wrong rhythms or pitches were played. Replay the tape and try to determine precisely what the errors were.

CONFERENCE: RP and Intervallic Illusions

The need to develop the ability to recall one or more RPs was mentioned earlier. This skill is invaluable when performing music that was composed with a clear tonal center. But there are musical compositions in all periods of music—perhaps more often in the nineteenth and twentieth centuries—where tonality is obscured by chromatic melodic figures or harmonies. In these cases the musician must hear abstract intervals, each tone becoming the RP for the following tone. You must be able to function then in two different musical environments: the tonal, in which basic and secondary RPs can be retained for considerable lengths of time; and the abstract, in which the RPs only last for a few tones. You must be able to shift from the tonal technique to the abstract in a moment.

Remember this fact, too: an interval is not often difficult in its isolated state, but the preceding pitch may "set it up," i.e., make it challenging aurally.

The following exercise will require you to hear abstract pitches. When you sing through it the first few times do not be concerned with rhythm. Hold each tone as long as you like until your inner ear hears the next pitch. Once you can sing the pitches try singing the exercise at different metronome speeds. Do not skip over the intervals that are difficult; these are the very places where you will benefit most.

Another fact worth pointing out is the *illusion* of expanding and contracting distance between intervals in certain melodic sequences. For example, when a series of whole tones are strung together there is the illusion that the farther one moves away from the first two whole tones the wider the pitches must be sung to keep the passage in tune.

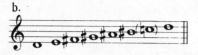

The same phenomenon happens when other successive, like intervals are sung, e.g., major thirds. Notice that the second M3 seems wider than the first.

An illusion of shortening the distance between intervals can be heard in the following examples. The half steps have the sensation of being closer after the series of whole tones.

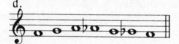

When singing ascending melodic lines you should have the feeling of singing a little higher for each note; and in descending melodic lines do not drop down quite so far.

In singing chromatic scale passages it is sometimes possible to retain the diatonic scale in the inner ear and not treat the chromatic notes as passing notes. Sing the example below as a diatonic scale (white notes); then add the "black notes" while thinking of the diatonic scale. You could practice this example singing the white notes *forte* and the black notes *piano*.

Tape 3-8____Aural Recognition: Review of Intervals

Write M3, m2, etc., after each interval that is heard.

After identifying the intervals go back and write in the correct notes on the staff. If you can, write in the notes on first hearing.

Descending Melodic Intervals

Ascending Melodic Intervals

Harmonic Intervals (Upper Note Given)

Harmonic Intervals (Lower Note Given)

MAJOR SCALES

The most frequently used scale in Western music has been the *major scale* with its semitones between the third and fourth and between the seventh and eighth degrees.

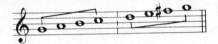

Notice that the first tetrachord (first four tones) has the same intervallic relationships as the second tetrachord.

Music using the major scale is so common in our everyday lives that we often assume it to be the norm for all music. This bias is not only too narrow to account for non-Western music; it does not take into account many, many pieces in the Western tradition.

In studying and comparing scales, the essential information is the location of particular intervals. Since the half step has a *leading* quality it is a particularly sensitive interval in any scale. As the various scales are learned, remember where the half steps occur in each.

MINOR SCALES

From the study of music theory you have learned that the minor scale has three forms. The variation is in the interval structure and can readily be perceived aurally, especially in melodic contexts.

Note that all forms have the same first (lower) five scale degrees. The variations occur at the higher end of the scale, in the sixth and seventh degrees.

The natural and melodic forms will be stressed first; the harmonic minor scale includes an augmented interval not discussed yet.

Exercise 3-3　Intonation: Minor Scales

Dynamics

Every musician should be familiar with the symbols used to indicate relative loudness or softness.

pp	pianissimo	very soft
p	piano	soft
mp	mezzo piano	rather soft
mf	mezzo forte	rather loud
f	forte	loud
ff	fortissimo	very loud

Instrumentalists know how to produce the various shades of loudness or softness on their instruments. However, since this book regularly uses the voice,

the nonsingers may have some difficulty making all six distinctions. For the present, concentrate on only two dynamics: *p* and *f*.

In performing exercises involving dynamics, keep in mind that the loudness or softness is as much a part of the "right note" as the pitch or rhythm. Sing the correct dynamics at the outset rather than adding them later.

Dynamics are written below the staff in instrumental music and above the staff in vocal music (to leave space for the text).

REHEARSED RHYTHM

Perform the following exercises at the indicated metronome settings and dynamics.

REHEARSED MELODIES

CONFERENCE: Ensembles

Ensemble pieces are designed to accomplish two objectives: to develop your awareness of the skills at work in ensemble participation and to develop your ability to read and hear open score. The following procedures are recommended:

1. Learn every part and be able to switch back and forth in performance.

2. Learn to see and hear in two directions: horizontally for melodic and vertically for harmonic.

Remember, if you cannot hear and sing the parts individually you will never be able to hear them simultaneously.

ENSEMBLES

SIGHT-READING

Handel, *Dettingen Te Deum*

Mexico

Brahms, *German Requiem*

MORE DIFFICULT

DICTATION

Tape 3-9____Rhythm

Melodic Motives

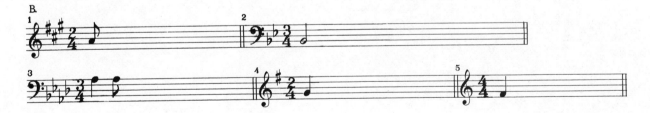

Melody

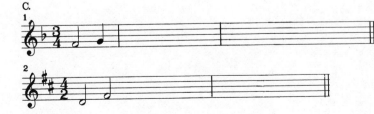

For additional practice with dictation replay Tape
3-2. Starting notes are given below.

UNIT 4

RHYTHM

Level 4 (Simple Subdivision)

At Level 2 the count is divided in halves; if the count is divided into quarters we are at rhythmic Level 4.

Level 4 rhythms are among the most common; therefore, every musician must work to completely master the variety of rhythms available at this level. At Level 2 there were only two possible combinations:

The possibilities for variety at Level 4 are more numerous. Consider the ways in which the sum of four can be reached.

```
1 + 1 + 1 + 1
2 +     1 + 1
1 + 2 +     1
1 + 1 + 2
2 +     2
1 + 3
3 +         1
```

Converting these sums into note values, we obtain these rhythms:

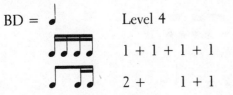

BD = ♩		Level 4
		1 + 1 + 1 + 1
		2 + 1 + 1

	1 + 2 + 1
	1 + 1 + 2
	2 + 2
	1 + 3
	3 + 1

Exercise 4-1   Note Values: Rhythm

By filling in the appropriate rhythms, complete similar charts with BD = ♪ and BD = ♩.

	BD = ♪	BD = ♩
1 + 1 + 1 + 1		
2 + 1 + 1		♩ ♫
1 + 2 + 1		
1 + 1 + 2		
2 + 2		
1 + 3		
3 + 1		

REHEARSED RHYTHM

Level 4: Ratios

Since Level 4 rhythms are so important, they will be taken up one at a time. Practice until you can perform these rhythms fluently.

Ratio: 1 + 1 + 1 + 1 

a. 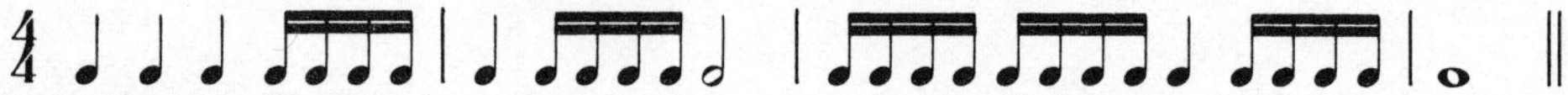

b. 

c. 

Ratio: 2 + 1 + 1 

d. 

e. 

f. 

Ratio: 1 + 2 + 1 

g. 

h. 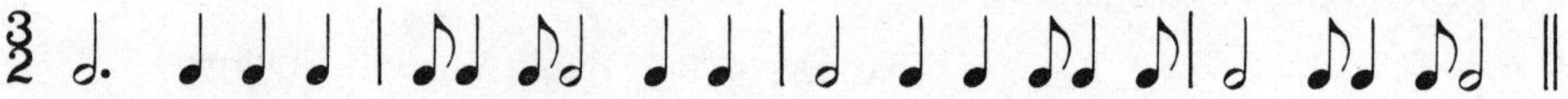

i. 

Ratio: 1 + 1 + 2 

j. 

k. 

l. 

Ratio: 2 + 2 

These rhythms are the same as Level 2.

Ratio: 1 + 3 

Special attention should be paid to performing Level 4 rhythms in which the first element is a rest.

These should be carefully practiced, sometimes followed by the next pulse,

and sometimes repeating the same rhythm.

As with Level 2 rhythms, accuracy can best be assured by practicing these rhythms as though they were at Level 1, i.e., shift the count so that the shortest note value receives a pulse.

Exercise 4-2   Note Values: Rhythm

Rewrite the following exercises, changing the value representing the BD as indicated.

b.

If the tempo indications are observed, there is no audible change in the music. However, you may find the visual change significant. Notice that the beams connecting the ♪ , ♪ , and ♫ help identify quickly Level 4 rhythms.

a.

b.

c.

Tape 4-1___Imitation with Notation: Rhythm

Listen to the rhythm performed in measure one while watching the notation. In measure two imitate the rhythm you just heard.

♩ = 69

Listen   Imitate   Listen   Imitate

a.

♩ = 69

b.

♩ = 60

c.

Write an X over places that are not performed as notated. If possible, write the rhythms that were performed.

a.

b.

c.

d.

e.

CONFERENCE: Practicing Rhythm

An ideal time to practice rhythm is while walking; your footsteps become a natural metronome. The time elapsing between each step will be one BD.

Practice rhythms you find difficult.

Practice shifting levels.

An awareness of rhythmic level is of great importance in practice and performance. To practice slowly without attention to rhythmic level may actually be detrimental, for reducing a tempo too much may bring it to the point where accuracy becomes more difficult to achieve. Slow practice makes sense only if it is coupled with an awareness of rhythmic level: slow the tempo and/or shift the count accordingly—this combination might produce beneficial results. Sometimes the tempo does not need to be slowed to improve accuracy; a shift of rhythmic level will suffice.

Exercise 4-3   Rehearsed Rhythm

Practice these Level 4 rhythms until you can perform them with no hesitation. If you have trouble with a particular passage, shift to Level 2.

INTERVALS

Perfect Fourth

To the eye the *perfect fourth* (P4) has an unsystematic appearance since it begins on a *line* and ends on a *space,* or begins on a *space* and ends on a *line.*

When sounded harmonically the P4 possesses an "open" sonority. The upper tone dominates; it is the root of the interval. Melodicaly, the ascending P4 is one of the most distinctive intervals. Many melodies beginning with an upbeat skip a P4 to the downbeat.

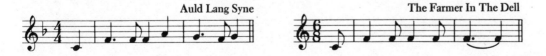

How many P4s are there in the major scale when fourths are built on each step of the scale, either descending or ascending?

Tape 4-3____Listening: Perfect Fourth

Listen to this series of P4s and learn their special qualities when they are played melodically (distance) and harmonically (sonority).

Tape 4-4____Tonal Memory

You will hear a group of five tones followed by a pause. During the pause, sing the tones you heard. The tape will then play the tones you should have sung.

Exercise 4-4   Visual Recognition of Intervals

Set your metronome at 104. Allow four pulses per measure, two pulses between measures. Refer back to Unit 3 if you do not recall how this exercise should be done.

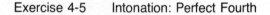

Exercise 4-5   Intonation: Perfect Fourth

Drone

48

Tape 4-5 ____ Imitation with Notation: Intervals

Repeat the interval sounded on the tape.

Tape 4-6 ____ Anticipation: Intervals

After the tape has sounded the RP, sing the interval indicated. The tape will repeat so you can check accuracy.

Tape 4-7 ____ Fusing: Perfect Fourth

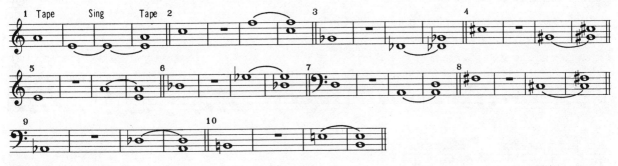

Review of Intervals

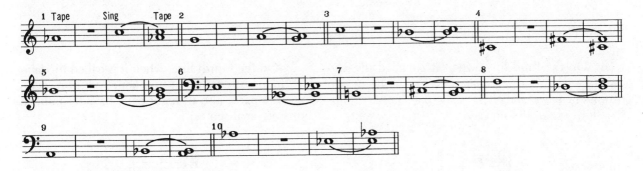

Tape 4-8____Aural Recognition: Intervals

Identify each of the ten intervals with an appropriate abbreviation, i.e., M3, m2, P4.

Melodic

1	2	3	4	5
6	7	8	9	10

Harmonic

1	2	3	4	5
6	7	8	9	10

Tape 4-9____Error Correction: Intervals

Five melodic and five harmonic intervals will be played. Indicate when they are incorrect while comparing them to the score. The first note in melodic intervals and the lower note in harmonic intervals will always be correct. Replay the tape if necessary. If you can, identify the exact interval sounded in measures with errors.

Tape 4-10____Error Correction: Melody

Study this melody before playing the tape. Circle and notate rhythmic and melodic errors.

The C Clef

The C clef appears in different locations on the staff:

1. On the third line, when it is called the *alto clef* (always found in viola parts, frequently in alto trombone parts, and often in alto parts in older publications of vocal scores).

2. On the fourth line, when it is called the *tenor clef* (frequently found in trombone, bassoon, cello, and bass parts; also in tenor parts in older publications of vocal scores).

50

The fastest way to read in C clef is to concentrate on a few "landmark" lines and spaces. *Do not transpose from treble (G clef) or bass clef (F clef)*. This added step will only confuse and delay your seeing and hearing in the C clef. Think alto or tenor clef from the very beginning. Learn these notes and then expand your range.

Exercise 4-6   Alto Clef

Only the alto clef will be introduced in this unit; the tenor clef will follow in Unit 5.

Be sure to identify the RP, carefully noting its position on the staff.

Exercise 4-7   Scanning

REHEARSED MELODIES

1 Con brio

2 Tauntingly

What is the tonality? Can you justify the key signature? What RP works best? Explain the last measure.

3 Allegro moderato

4 ♩ = 84   Note the key signature

5 Poco lento

52

CONFERENCE: Performing Ensembles

To be a good ensemble performer it is not enough merely to count your part accurately. You must listen as well to the other part(s) and make minute adjustments as needed to maintain precision in an ensemble. Slight *rubato* effects should not be difficult to accomplish in a duet or other small ensemble if all the performers are sensitive and careful.

As you sing these exercises let your eye move from your part to the other(s), so that you know what to expect and can adjust accordingly. Also, by watching the other parts you will gain insight into the music and sharpen your musical ear considerably. Performing artists in the finest vocal and instrumental chamber ensembles learn the parts of the other members of the ensemble almost as well as they do their own. Therefore, it is suggested that you learn both parts in these exercises and exchange at the beginning or even during a performance on signal from the teacher or student conductor.

ENSEMBLES

54

SIGHT-READING

MORE DIFFICULT

For the virtuoso. Set your own tempo.

Watch the intonation!

DICTATION

Tape 4-11___Rhythm

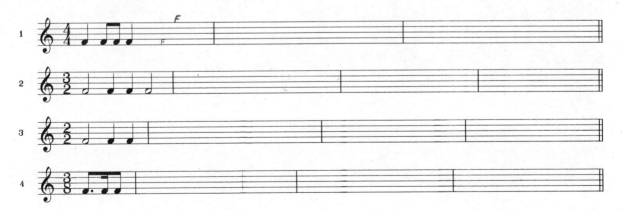

Motives.

First note is given. Listen to the entire motive before trying to write. Do not try to write and listen at the same time.

Tape 4-12_____Melody

A.

For additional practice replay Tape 4-4. Starting notes are given below.

B.

58

UNIT 5

RHYTHM

Level 3: Compound Meters

Level 1 dealt only with tones one or more counts in length. Levels 2 and 4 divided the counts in halves and quarters. This binary division is called *simple division*, and meters in which simple division is employed are called *simple meters*.

Meters in which the count is divided in thirds are called *compound meters*.

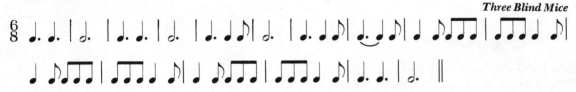

Three Blind Mice

At the beginning of this song all the tones are one or two BDs in length. If one did not see the notation there would be no way to distinguish whether the meter were *simple* or *compound*. But in measure five it becomes clear that the division is in thirds: the meter is *compound*.

Whether a piece is in simple or compound meter can only be determined by the presence of Level 2 or 3 rhythms or subdivisions of those levels. A composition in which Level 1 rhythms only are employed may be written as either simple or compound.

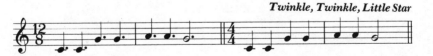

Twinkle, Twinkle, Little Star

Simple meter signatures present no difficulty. The rule is that the upper number indicates the number of beats to the measure and the lower number indicates the kind of note that gets a beat.

In compound meters the BD is represented by a dotted note, usually ♪. , ♩. , or ♩. . The simplicity of the modified meter signatures can now be more fully appreciated:

If these signatures are converted to traditional forms the simple meters become 4/4, 2/4, 3/8. The compound meters cannot be so simply converted, for there is no whole number that represents the dotted

Simple meters   Compound meters

59

note. Therefore, the tradition is to indicate the type of note that represents the *division*, not the BD, in which case the compound-meter signatures above would be $\frac{12}{8}$, $\frac{6}{16}$, $\frac{9}{4}$. *Simple-meter signatures indicate a typical measure at Level 1:* $\frac{4}{4}$ ♩ ♩ ♩ ♩. *Compound-meter signatures indicate a typical measure at Level 3:*

Exercise 5-1   Meter Signatures

Complete the following charts of meter signatures.

Simple Meters

If the BD is represented by	And there is 1 pulse to the measure the signature is	2 pulses to the measure	3	4	5	6
𝅗𝅥						
♩				$\frac{4}{4}$		
♪						

Compound Meters

If the BD is represented by	And there is 1 pulse to the measure the signature is	2 pulses to the measure	3	4	5	6
𝅗𝅥.						
♩.				$\frac{12}{8}$		
♪.						

Notice that certain signatures appear in both charts ($\frac{3}{4}$, $\frac{6}{8}$, etc.).

What is the difference between these two signatures?

Can the difference be heard in the music?

Level 3 Rhythms

Let us explore the possible rhythmic combinations at Level 3.

$$3$$
$$1 + 1 + 1$$
$$2 + \qquad 1$$
$$1 + 2$$

Converting these ratios to notated rhythms using the more common BD values we get

BD = 𝅗𝅥.		BD = ♩.		BD = ♪.		
♩	♩ ♩		♪♪♪		♬	1 + 1 + 1
𝅗𝅥	𝅗𝅥		♪ ♪		♪ ♪	1 + 2
𝅗𝅥	𝅗𝅥	♩ ♪		♪ ♪		2 + 1

Exercise 5-2   Rehearsed Rhythm

Perform these exercises. Each set employs a ratio frequently encountered in compound meters.

Ratio : 1 + 1 + 1

a. 9/8

b. 12/4

c. 9/16

Ratio : 2 + 1

d. 3/8

e. 6/4

f. 6/16

Ratio : 1 + 2

g. 12/8

h. 3/4

i. 9/16

Exercise 5-3   Meter Signatures

Indicate the meter of these folksongs.

	Simple or Compound	Number of BDs per measure
"On Top of Old Smokey"		
"Home on the Range"		
"Battle Hymn of the Republic"		
"Dixie"		
"Star-Spangled Banner"		
"Irish Washerwoman"		

Exercise 5-4   Note Values

Rewrite the following compound meters.

Complete the measures that have too few or too many notes or rests.

Tape 5-1___Anticipation: Rhythm

Establish the tempo.
Anticipate the rhythm of the following two measures.
Check your accuracy.

Tape 5-2___Error Correction: Rhythm

Mark an X in any measure that is not played as notated.

Exercise 5-5   Rehearsed Rhythm

As at Levels 2 and 4, if greater accuracy is desired practice these rhythms at Level 1.

Notice that the absence of beams in the last two examples makes the visual grouping of notes into BDs more difficult.

i. 𝅗𝅥.=60

j. 𝅗𝅥.=144

INTERVALS

Perfect Fifth

The *perfect fifth*, P5, has an orderly appearance on the staff. If the RP is on a line the P5 is either two lines above or below. Likewise, if the RP is on a space the P5 is two spaces above or below.

When the P5 is heard melodically there is an awareness of greater distance. It is the first of the larger intervals.

The P5 sounded harmonically has an open sonority. The element of close harmony experienced when hearing the M3 and m3 is absent. It is the openness of the P5 that causes confusion sometimes with the *perfect fourth*. Both intervals have open sonorities, but the distance of the P4 is not as wide.

Also, in the P5 the lower tone dominates, i.e., is the root of the interval.

Tape 5-3____Listening: Perfect Fifth

The intervals on this tape will be heard in this order:
  a. five perfect fifths, played melodically
     five perfect fifths, played harmonically
  b. comparison of perfect fourth and perfect fifth, played melodically (three sets)
  c. comparison of perfect fourth and perfect fifth, played harmonically (three sets)

Tape 5-4____Tonal Memory

Listen to the five-tone groups. Then sing the tones. The tape will then repeat the group.

Exercise 5-6   Visual Recognition: Intervals

Set the metronome at ♩=120. Cover the music. At each fourth pulse expose one measure and identify the interval.

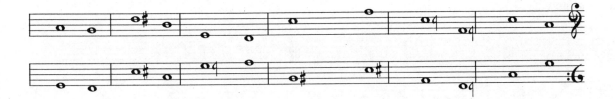

Exercise 5-7　　Intonation: Perfect Fifth

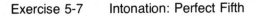

Tape 5-5____Imitation with Notation: Intervals

Each measure will be played twice. Listen the first time; sing with the tape, as notated, the second time.

Perfect Fifth

Review of Intervals

Tape 5-6____Anticipation: Intervals

An RP will be sounded in the first measure. In the second measure, sing the interval given. The tape will repeat in the third measure what you should have sung.

Observe that the first six exercises are concerned with the P5, while those that follow review other intervals.

Tape 5-7____Fusing

Perfect Fifth

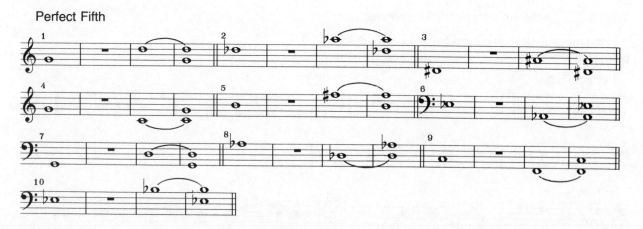

Review of Intervals

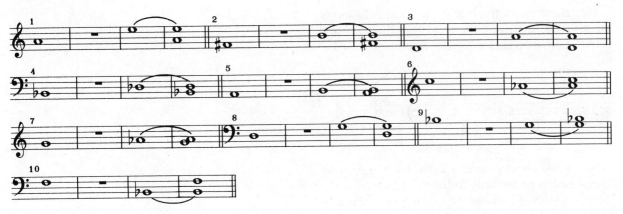

Tape 5-8_____Aural Recognition: Intervals

Identify the intervals played.

Melodic					Harmonic				
1	2	3	4	5	1	2	3	4	5
6	7	8	9	10	6	7	8	9	10

Tape 5-9_____Error Correction: Melody

Study this melody using the techniques recommended for Rehearsed Melodies. When you can hear it in your inner ear, play the tape. Circle and correct rhythmic and melodic errors on the printed version below.

HARMONY

Triads, like intervals, are basic experiences which must be practiced until they are thoroughly familiar. Since triads are more complex structures than intervals they require more extensive analysis.

There are three aspects of any triad which may be identified: (1) quality, (2) inversion, and (3) function.

Quality should always be the first identified. For the present, two qualities will be stressed: major and minor. The *dominant seventh chord* and the *diminished triad* will be introduced later in this book, while others will be delayed until the second volume.

Inversion of triads and chords will be taken up in later units of this book as will *function*, the relationship of harmonies to tonality.

Triads

Play these major triads at the keyboard. Listen to the *sonority*, then sing the root. Play the triad and listen again; then sing the third. Repeat, singing the fifth.

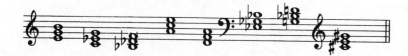

Repeat the above process with the following minor triads. Listen particularly to the third, which is the interval that distinguishes the major from the minor triad.

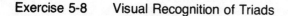

Exercise 5-8   Visual Recognition of Triads

Set your metronome at ♩ = 104. Allow four pulses to recognize whether the following triads are major or minor.

Exercise 5-9   Fusing: Major and Minor Triads

Play the root-position triad, major or minor, shown in measure one. Sing the sequence of pitches in measure two, in tune, repeating the triad drone as often as necessary.

When you can can sing the two kinds of triads accurately, practice these variations:

1. Sing them backwards (retrograde).

2. Sing with the steady pulse of the metronome, gradually increasing the speed each time. You will know you are hearing the triad if you can sing it in tune at a rapid tempo.

3. Compose melodic and rhythmic variations of the triad.

Exercise 5-10   Fusing: Triads

At the keyboard play the RP for each of the triads. After playing the RP try to hear the triad in your inner ear. Then play the triad to check your accuracy.

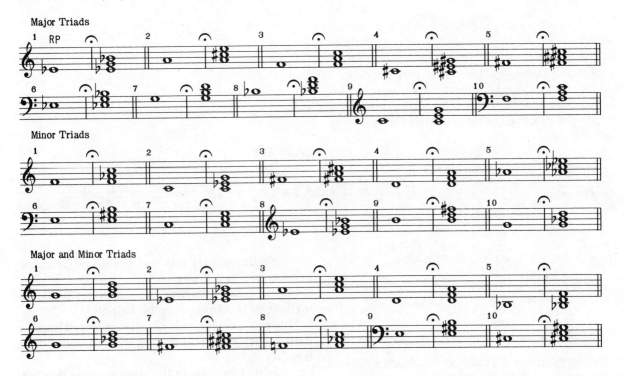

Exercise 5-11   Major and Minor Triads

Play only the white note. Find the other pitches from this note, then sing the triad (Exercise 5-9.)

Tape 5-10____Aural Recognition: Triads

Indicate with M or m whether each triad is major or minor.

1	2	3	4	5
6	7	8	9	10
11	12	13	14	15

Tape 5-11____Error Correction: Triads

In each example, the root of the triad is shown correctly. Listen to it and determine if other accidentals are needed or if the triad is right as it appears.

Two-Part Music: Parallel, Similar, Contrary, and Oblique Motion

Up to this point, ear-training studies have been limited to identifying isolated, single harmonic intervals. A succession of harmonic intervals may give rise to a harmonic or contrapuntal passage, depending on whether one hears vertical sonorities or two (horizontal) melodic parts. The relative motion of two parts is described by the terms *parallel*, *contrary*, and *oblique*.

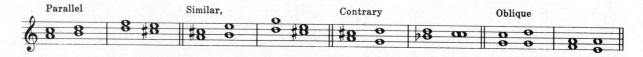

Tape 5-12____Listening: Two-Part Music

You will hear five examples each of parallel, contrary, and oblique motion.

Tape 5-13____Aural Recognition: Two-Part Music

On this tape you will hear ten examples similar to those on Tape 5-12 except that the types will be mixed. Indicate by P, C, or O the type of motion heard in each.

1	2	3	4	5
6	7	8	9	10

CONFERENCE: Two-Part Music.

While listening to Tape 5-14 be aware of two factors: the harmonic intervals formed by the parts, and the motion of each separate part. The relative motion, if not perceived directly, can be deduced from the sonorities and melodic motion.

If you are still having trouble identifying the various intervals studied up to this point, it is imperative that you do everything possible to remedy this deficiency. Without the ability to identify harmonic intervals there is no way to become proficient at hearing two-part music.

When learning to hear two (or more) parts this method of practicing may be helpful:

Sing each part melodically. If you cannot hear the parts separately it will be impossible to hear them together.

Fuse the two parts in the same manner that harmonic intervals and chords have been fused in former units. The following example

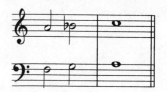

can be fused several ways:

1. lower to upper note of each pulse;
2. upper to lower note of each pulse;
3. a mixture of the previous two.

It may prove useful to practice the parts as though they were in the same octave. When you are sure of this, work at hearing the parts in the notated register.

When this has been accomplished switch to hearing the series mentally as vertical sonorities. Do not be discouraged if it does not happen immediately.

Tape 5-14——Error Correction: Two-Part Music

Before listening to this tape, rehearse these exercises in your inner ear—without playing them on an instrument. Use the techniques suggested in the conference.

1. When the tape is played, mark an X in the measures that are not performed as written.

2. Replay the tape and write the correct notes in those measures where there are errors.

Exercise 5-12   Tenor Clef

The brief melodies given below are designed to introduce you to the tenor clef. There are few skips and the pitches gravitate around middle C on the fourth line of the staff. Again, pick out a few landmark notes, then expand your range.

Exercise 5-13   Scanning

REHEARSED MELODIES

German Folksong

Allegretto ♪ = 126   What rythmic level?

In this melody it will be helpful to keep three RP's in mind

Michael Cavendish

Andante

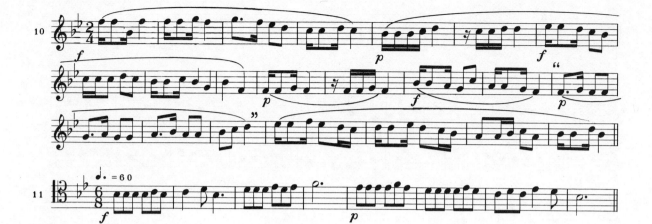

ENSEMBLES

Haydn, *Lord Nelson Mass "Credo"*

Monteverdi

MORE DIFFICULT
(Melodies for the Bolder Student)

If you can do #2, ask a friend to sing the following with you as a duet, i.e., #2 and #3 together.

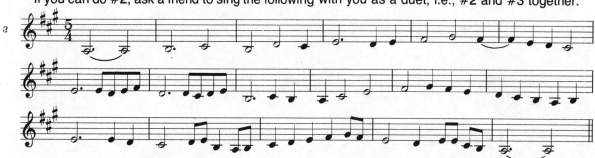

DICTATION

Tape 5-15____Rhythm

Complete the notation of each example.

d. $\frac{12}{8}$ ♪♪♪ | | ‖

e. $\frac{9}{4}$ ♩ ♩ | | ‖

Tape 5-16___Motives

A.

Melody

B.

For additional practice, replay Tape 5-5. Starting notes are given below.

C.

Tape 5-17_____Two-Part Music

The upper part is given in the two-part exercises
shown below. Write the lower part from what you
hear.

UNIT 6

INTERVALS

Sixths—Major and Minor

As melodic intervals become larger the sense of space that they cover becomes prominent. The sixths are "large" intervals; in singing and hearing them one has the feeling of wide distances.

Like other intervals, the *major* and *minor sixths* (M6 and m6) have their own sonorities when sounded harmonically and their own feeling of distance when heard melodically. There is also an interesting phenomenon that becomes more obvious with inter-vals larger than the perfect fifth. The sense of a skip or gap is so great when the larger intervals are used that there is a natural tendency for melodies to fill in some of the space immediately. It is as though the large skip creates a kind of melodic vacuum which requires filling. Note in the following melodies how the large skip is filled in by motion in the opposite direction.

As a result, the sixth may be heard and performed as though one of the tones is a neighbor to the fifth.

Sometimes a melodic figure may be perceived and performed as though the large skips are formed of neighbor tones to an RP taken from the tonal structure of the melody. In the following figures one need not hear the interval of the sixth to sing the note B; one may find the B by using the final note C as the RP.

Of course, one often encounters the sixth in melodic figures that are less common than the above cliché. In those cases one must be able to hear and sing the absolute interval. As your skill in reading develops you will be able to determine very quickly if there is a useful RP in a particular passage or if you will need to hear the abstract interval.

Tape 6-1____Listening: Sixths

The intervals on this tape will be heard in this order:
   a. five major sixths, played melodically
      five major sixths, played harmonically
   b. five minor sixths, played melodically
      five minor sixths, played harmonically
   c. comparison of major and minor sixth, played melodically (three sets)
   d. comparison of major and minor sixth, played harmonically (three sets)

Visually, it is easy to confuse the major and minor sixths since the distance from the RP is wide. Therefore, in the early stages of recognition of these inter-

vals it is not uncommon for students to find a visual shortcut. Picture a P5, then count a M2 beyond for the M6, or a m2 for the m6.

You may also find it useful to think of the inversion of the interval, i.e., think of the upper note as though it were an octave lower.

Eventually, the musician should memorize all the diatonic and chromatic combinations of notes that make up the two kinds of sixths. Response to what is seen must be instantaneous.

Exercise 6-1   Visual Recognition: Sixths

Set the metronome at 100. Identify each interval within four pulses.

Tape 6-2____Tonal Memory

You will hear a series of six tones. During the rest that follows, sing the six tones. The tape will repeat so you can check your accuracy.

Tape 6-3____Imitation with Notation: Sixths

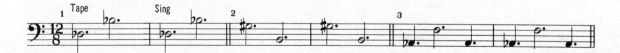

Exercise 6-2   Intonation: Sixths

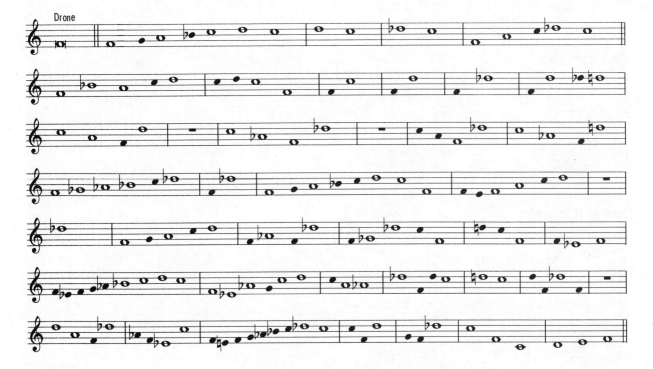

CONFERENCE: Timbre and Interval Recognition

Timbre can have interesting effects on sonority. For example, there is the phenomenon of timbre causing the ear to "invert" played or sung intervals. This experience takes place: (1) when the timbre of the lower voice or instrument has stronger overtones than the upper part; (2) when the top part is written in a low range (tessitura) and the lower part in a high range; and (3) when both (1) and (2) are interacting.

The effects of timbre can be seen in the examples below where the "white" notes are performed pitches and the "black" notes indicate the *inverted* sonorities that are frequently but mistakenly heard. (Voices and instruments are at concert pitch.)

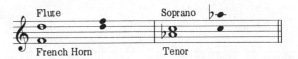

Although *thirds* and *sixths* are shown above, the phenomenon is common to all intervals.

Timbre can also affect the dissonant qualities of intervals, particularly *seconds* and *sevenths*.

Tape 6-4 ___ Anticipation: Sixths; Review of Intervals

Review of Intervals

Tape 6-5 ___ Fusing

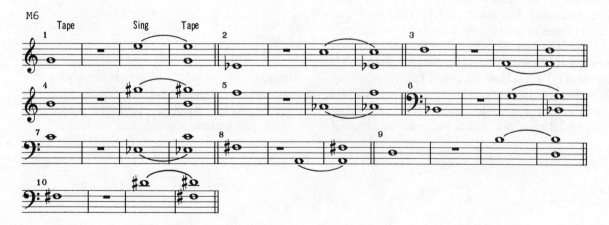

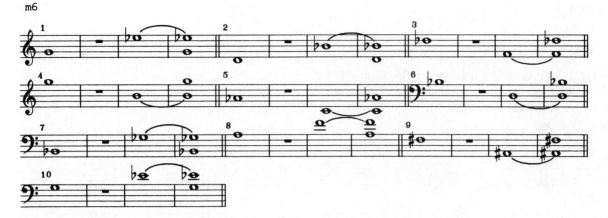

Review of Intervals

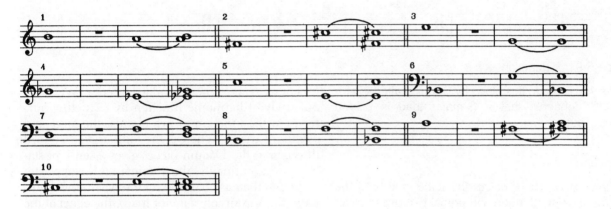

Tape 6-6___Aural Recognition: Review of Intervals

Write the appropriate symbol after each interval that is played.

Melodic

1	2	3	4	5
6	7	8	9	10

Harmonic

1	2	3	4	5
6	7	8	9	10

Tape 6-7___Error Correction: Melody

Learn the following melody using the inner ear, then play the tape, circling errors in the performance. If an incorrect dynamic or accent is heard, consider these as errors, too. Replay the tape if necessary to define the exact nature of the errors.

Hungarian Folksong

Tape 6-8____Anticipation: Major and Minor Triads

The first pitch you will hear will be the RP. From this RP hear the triad shown in measure two. The tape will then play the triad so you can check the accuracy of your inner ear.

Tape 6-9____Function

As you listen to this piece by Daquin called "Tambourin," observe that a G-major triad is played throughout.

Function

Once your ear perceives the static quality of the harmony your attention will probably move to other aspects of the piece—for example, the melody and rhythm. The effect of this Daquin work may remind you of an intonation exercise.

In most music, however, the harmony changes: it functions as an element of added interest. We begin our study of harmonic function by restricting ourselves to the function of two chords, the *tonic* and *dominant* triads. Whereas the tonic triad, sounded throughout the Daquin piece, gives a sense of stability, rest, or finality, the dominant is the opposite. Although there is no dissonant interval in the dominant (the V is simply a major triad), the effect of the dominant is of tension requiring a return to the tonic or a sense of incompleteness that needs resolution. This is caused largely by the presence of the *leading tone,* the third of the V triad.

Exercise 6-3   Fusing: Tonic and Dominant

Sing the following melodic exercise, which emphasizes the tonic and dominant qualities. As you can see, it is an elaboration of Exercise 5-7.

When you have completed the elaboration, try to hear the I and V triads as vertical sonorities.

Exercise 6-4   Anticipation: Review of Major and Minor Triads

Play the following triad roots at the keyboard, then try to hear the quality of the triad indicated. When you are positive you have a mental image of the quality, play the triad to check. Repeat this exercise until you can do it with no errors.

Repeat this exercise, calling the RP the third or fifth of the triad.

Tape 6-10___Anticipation: Tonic and Dominant

The tape will play a tonic triad in major or minor.

Sing or hear the dominant triad notated in the second measure.

The tape will then play the dominant so you can verify your answer.

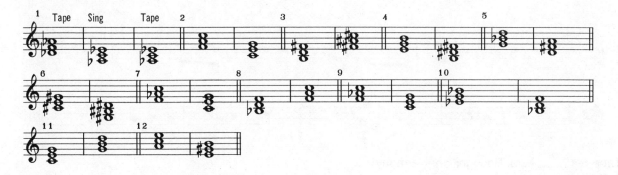

Spacing

Spacing, sometimes called *voicing*, is another compositional technique that produces nuances of color and texture that should be pointed out in the study of ear training. The examples below demonstrate several spacings, redistributions of the notes of the same chord, and how these shifts modify the aural results. Perform these exercises in class on the piano, singing (SATB), and with different instrumental groupings and discover how the spacings vary in texture and color.

Exercise 6-5   Spacing

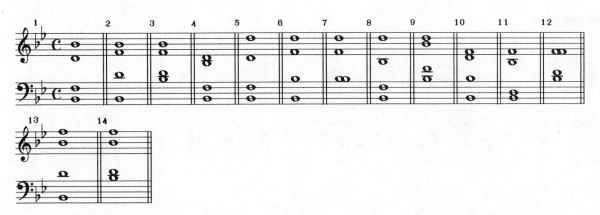

Three melodies are given below. The first is written out completely, while only the melody line is given for the second and third; however, all three will be performed in the same way. First you will hear the melody played unaccompanied. It will then be repeated with a simple bass part of tonic and dominant tones. Finally the melody will be played with the bass part and full harmony.

Tape 6-12____Aural Recognition: Harmony

An accompaniment has been added to a melody that you learned in Unit 4. Indicte the harmony changes by writing I or V below the staff. A "+" indicates a *non-chord tone,* a note not part of the prevailing harmony, which creates a momentary dissonance.

New melodies.

Exercise 6-6   Harmonizing Folksongs

Using only the I and V triads, accompany yourself at the keyboard or guitar in these two folksongs.

Down in the Valley

The Bridge at Avignon

Exercise 6-7   Fusing: Two-Part Music

The eight-measure two-part piece below is designed to help you develop your ability to hear counterpoint in the inner ear.

Unit 5 has an explanation of the techniques that should be utilized in learning this skill (see p.70).

Practice until you can hear the entire piece.

Accents

There are various types of accents in music. One of the most important is the *agogic* accent, which is the normal accent that occurs on a longer note surrounded by shorter notes. Thus, in

one feels an accent on the quarter note even if one carefully sings all the notes at the same volume.

Sometimes the composer wishes to place accents in places not normally accented, or he may choose to have a particular note performed louder than others around it. This is called a *dynamic accent*. Unless otherwise indicated, the tone with an accent marked > should be performed at one dynamic level higher than the prevailing dynamic at the time.

indicates

For more extreme accents the composer may indicate *fp* or *sfz*.

From this point on, the full range of dynamics
from *pp* to *ff* will be found in our exercises. Gauge
your vocal dynamic range so that there is a difference
between *f* and *ff*, *mf* and *mp*.

RHYTHM

Meter Changes

Sometimes a change of meter involves a change in
the BD; we will consider these cases later. For the
present we will consider meter changes in which the
length of the BD is not affected; only the number of
BDs in the measure varies.

The Twelve Days Of Christmas

No change of tempo is implied here because ♩ = ♩

Exercise 6-8   Rehearsed Rhythm: Accents and Meter Changes

90

Exercise 6-9   Scanning

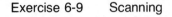

REHEARSED MELODIES

Hungarian Melody

English Melody

This melody will be used again in a later unit.

© Copyright Oxford University Press, London
Used by permission of the publisher.

Richard Rodney Bennett, *Sweet was the Song, Five Carols*

© Copyright 1967 by Universal Edition (London) Ltd., London. Used by permission of the publisher.

Cuba-Mexico

ENSEMBLES

Praetorius

Schuetz

SIGHT-READING

Purcell, *Come Ye Sons of Art*

A. Scarlatti, *Christmas Cantata*

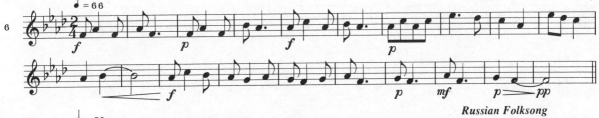

Russian Folksong

Mozart, *Mass in C, Gloria, K. 337*

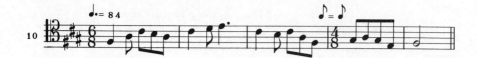

MORE DIFFICULT

DICTATION

Tape 6-13 ____Rhythm

The number of measures in each example is omitted deliberately. Mark in the barlines.

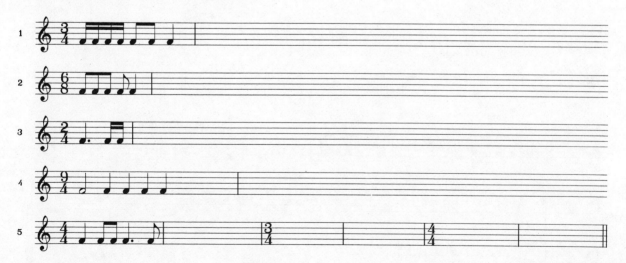

Tape 6-14___Motives

A.

Melody

B.

For additional dictation replay Tape 6-2. Starting
notes are given below.

C.

Tape 6-15____Two-Part Music

Tempo di marcia   Jeremiah Clarke

Tape 6-16____Harmony

Write the soprano and bass parts and the chord symbols.

UNIT 7

INTERVALS

Sevenths—Major and Minor

Sevenths are readily identified on the staff. If the RP is on a space the seventh is three spaces above or below; if on a line, the seventh is three lines above or below the RP.

Until all the sevenths have been memorized and can be identified at a glance, an intermediate method is to count inward from the RP's octave, a whole step for the m7 and a half step for the M7.

Aurally the M7 has a biting, dissonant sound, comparable to the m2 and tritone. The m7 is less dissonant, comparable to the M2.

Exercise 7-1   Visual Recognition of Major and Minor Sevenths

Set metronome at 92 and allow four pulses for each interval.

Review of Intervals

Tape 7-1____Listening: Sevenths

The intervals on this tape will be heard in this order:
a. five minor sevenths, played melodically
five minor sevenths, played harmonically
b. five major sevenths, played melodically
five major sevenths, played harmonically
c. comparison of minor and major seventh,
played melodically (three sets)
d. comparison of minor and major seventh,
played harmonically (three sets)

Tape 7-2____Tonal Memory

A series of seven tones will be played. Immediately after the tape plays the tones, try to sing back as many as possible. The tones will then be repeated.

Tape 7-3____Imitation with Notation

Listen as the tape plays the notes in each measure.
Sing when the tape repeats each measure.

Exercise 7-2   Intonation

Tape 7-4____Anticipation: Sevenths

Minor seventh

Major seventh

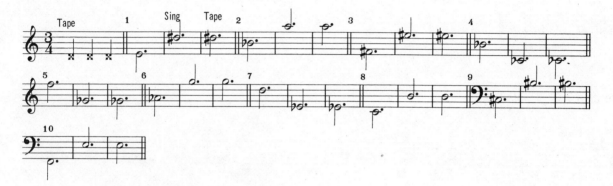

Tape 7-5____Anticipation: Review of Intervals

Tape 7-6____Fusing

Major seventh

A.

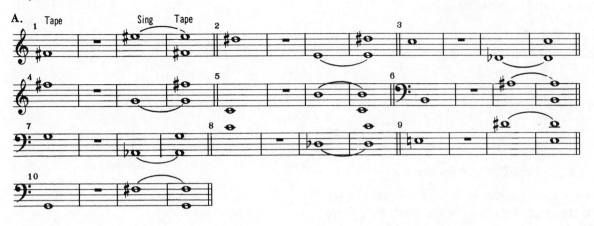

Minor seventh

B.

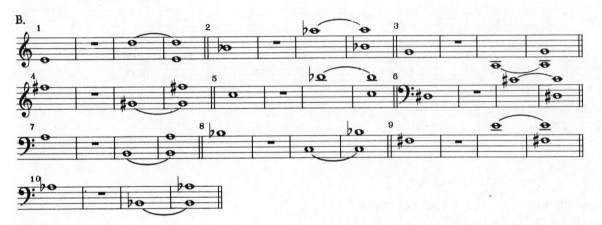

Review of Intervals

C.

Melodic and Harmonic Sevenths

1	2	3	4	5
6	7	8	9	10

Melodic Review

1	2	3	4	5
6	7	8	9	10

Harmonic Review

1	2	3	4	5
6	7	8	9	10

Tape 7-8____Error Correction: Intervals

If the written interval is not the interval played, correct the second pitch. (The first pitch will always be correct.)

Tape 7-9____Error Correction: Melody

Mark those measures where you hear errors, then identify the wrong rhythm or pitch. Write in the correct rhythms or pitches.

English Folksong

HARMONY

Subdominant Function

In the previous unit the tonic and dominant functions were introduced. Another basic function that must be added to a harmonic vocabulary is the *subdominant*. It is this triad that is clearly heard in the IV-I (plagal) cadence at the end of numerous hymns, the "Amen." Aurally, the I-IV or IV-I progression has a mellower, less intense effect when compared to the I-V or V-I.

104

Tape 7-10____Listening: Harmony—Subdominant

When listening to this tape compare the tonic-subdominant-tonic progression and the tonic-dominant-tonic progression in both the major and minor. Also, note the function of the subdominant when it precedes the dominant.

1. I   IV I
2. I   V   I
3. i   iv i
4. i   V   i
5. I   IV V   I
6. i   iv V   i

CONFERENCE: Fusing Parts

The fusing exercise that follows is designed to make the transition from hearing a triadic progression in its melodic form to hearing it in its harmonic form.

When you can sing No. 1 flawlessly in a slow tempo, increase the tempo gradually until each measure can be heard at a tempo that becomes too rapid to sing and, consequently, can only be heard in the inner ear. This process is called "tilting"; the faster the inner ear hears the melodic version (No. 1) the more the sonorities tilt from a horizontal (melodic) experience to a vertical (harmonic) experience (No. 2).

Exercise 7-3   Fusing: Function of Major and
        Minor Triads

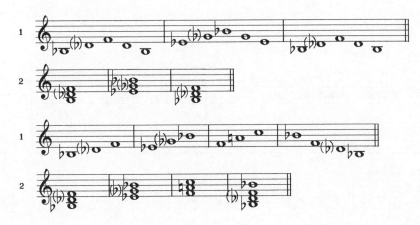

Soprano Factors

The sonority of a chord changes when different factors are placed in the soprano. The only way to learn to identify these is through repeated listening; each sonority is distinct. The process of identifying the soprano tone in a chord may be related to identifying the starting pitch in melodic dictation.

In the following exercise listen to the soprano part; relate it to the root of the chord. Listen for the inflections as the chord positions change.

Each example will be played twice; first in major, then in minor.

Tape 7-11_____Listening: Factors

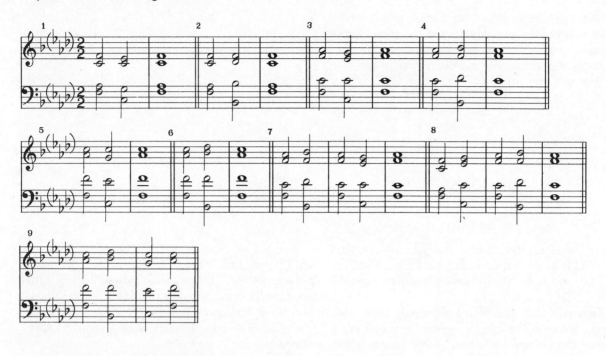

Tape 7-12_____Listening: Harmony—Subdominant

1. An unaccompanied melody will be played first.
2. When it is played again the melody will be accompanied by a bass part which will imply the underlying I, IV, or V triads.
3. The third time the melody will be fully harmonized.

CONFERENCE: Polyphony

When dealing with an unaccompanied melody our concern is for the manner in which tones relate to each other in succession.

Similarly, in part music the tones of each *separate* part relate melodically to one another in the same way as in monophony. But because the other part is sounding at the same time the relationships *between* the parts brings a whole new dimension to the music. Therefore, in part music our concern for intervals is not only for the melodic intervals of each part but also for the harmonic intervals formed by the simultaneous melodies. The combination of parts creates a musical texture which is more complex than the "sum of the parts." In addition to the melodic lines themselves, there is the interest of the harmonic intervals, the interaction of the rhythm of the two parts, and the harmonic background.

Take for example the following melody

to be combined with this melody.

Melody A is somewhat stronger, more commanding of our attention, but both A and B have their own pitch structure and contour. The rhythms of the two seem similar; however, they are not identical. When performed together the accented pulses clearly coincide and the harmonic intervals imply an obvious harmonic background.

Suppose we substitute this melody for B:

Here we have a melody which offers more competition to the A. Although the accents still coincide and the implied harmony is the same, the effect is one of more independence of the parts. The emotional impact of this combination is more conflicted and urgent.

The potentially enormous complexity of part music must be coupled with some regard for human limitations; our attention cannot be directed simultaneously to melody A, melody B, the harmonic intervals resulting, *and* the implied harmonic background—not to mention the variety of rhythmic relationships between the parts.

It is because of this complexity that the inner ear cannot grasp everything at once; this is why we like to hear music many times. We frequently hear things we did not hear before.

In view of this problem you must be patient in developing your ear. Some people hear implied harmony better than others. If your recognition of intervals is not secure you will have added difficulty.

Another fact to remember is one that was mentioned earlier: if you cannot hear the individual parts in two-part music you will not be able to hear them together.

When listening, allow your attention to jump back and forth through the polyphonic texture to grasp as much as you can. If you find that you can only hear one melody, force yourself to listen to the other part (fusing will help) or to the harmonic background.

Be patient, but persistent. Your ear *will* develop!

RHYTHM

Exercise 7-4   Scanning

REHEARSED RHYTHM

Intone the following exercises at the tempos indicated.

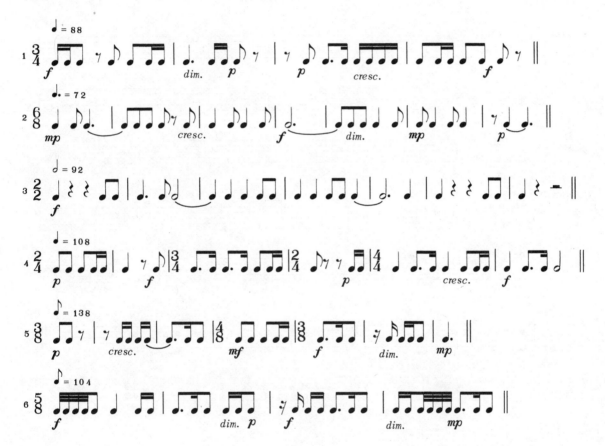

REHEARSED MELODIES

Schumann

Alec Wilder, *"Lowland Sea"*

© Copyright by G. Schirmer, Inc., New York.
Used by permission of the publisher.

ENSEMBLES

112

MORE DIFFICULT

Tape 7-13____Error Correction: Two-Part Music

The two-part example printed below is one you learned in Unit 3 under Ensembles (No. 5).

In listening to this tape, try to hear both parts simultaneously. This may necessitate a little review; singing the parts separately, then fusing them before playing the tape.

Mark an X where rhythmic or melodic errors occur. Try to identify the mistakes in specific terms in later replays.

DICTATION

Tape 7-14____Rhythm

A.

Melody

For additional dictation replay Tape 7-2. Starting notes are given below.

C.

CONFERENCE: Two-Part Music

At first hearing the two-part dictation example that follows might seem formidable, but in reality it is not difficult. Recall the suggestions given for melodic dictation in Unit 2 (p. 24) and apply them to two-part dictation. Of course, the significant difference is disciplining yourself to hear the two parts horizontally and vertically at the same time.

Do not be in too much of a hurry to write until the music is played several times. Look for rhythmic and melodic repetitions as well as important harmonic intervals. If you avoid listening to the two parts simultaneously you will delay your mastery of this skill.

Tape 7-15____Two-Part Music

Tape 7-16____Harmony

Write the soprano and bass parts and the chord
symbols.

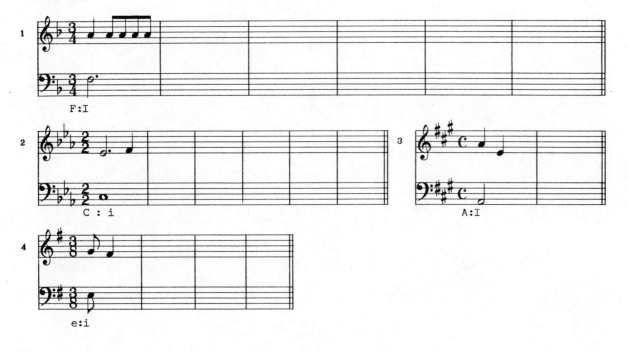

UNIT 8

INTERVALS

Tritone

The *tritone* (T) appears as an *augmented fourth*, A4, or as a *diminished fifth*, d5. Both contain six half steps.

This resolution pattern is also reflected in melodic passages, for example:

The foregoing examples show that scale degrees 4 and 7 have tendencies to resolve to 3 and 8 respectively.

Since the tritone is comparable in dissonant quality

to the M7, special attention must be given to this interval, particularly when the tonality is not clear.

Out of context, it is impossible to differentiate aurally between the A4 and d5. However, in a particular tonality the ear calculates which scale degrees are involved: 4 to 7 (A4), 7 to 4 (d5).

Harmonically the tritone is dissonant and implies a resolution; if the interval is augmented the resolution is *outward*, if diminished, the resolution is *inward*.

Tape 8-1___Listening: Tritone

Twelve tritones will be played in various registers, the first six melodically, the last six harmonically.

Tape 8-2___Tonal Memory

Groups of seven tones. Try to sing back all seven.

Tape 8-3___Imitation with Notation: Tritone

Each of the twelve items will be played twice. Imitate the interval during the repetition. Check intonation.

Exercise 8-1   Visual Recognition: Intervals

With the metronome set at 100 identify the following intervals within four pulses. If this is too easy, try three.

Exercise 8-2   Intonation: Tritone

Tape 8-4_____Anticipation: Tritone

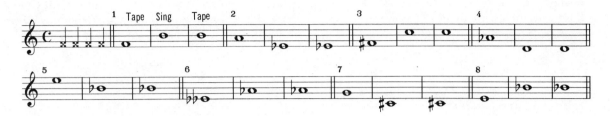

Tape 8-5_____Fusing: Tritone, Review of Intervals

A.
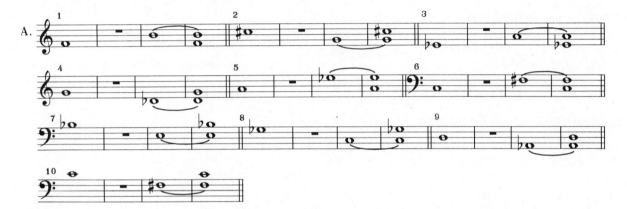

Review of Intervals

B.
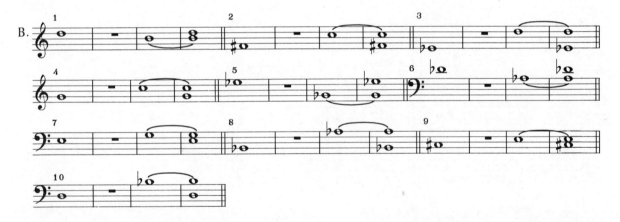

Tape 8-6_____Aural Recognition: Review of Intervals

Using T to represent the tritone, and other symbols learned previously, identify the following intervals.

Melodic

1	2	3	4	5
6	7	8	9	10

Harmonic

1	2	3	4	5
6	7	8	9	10

Tape 8-7_____Error Correction: Review of Intervals

Mark an X on those intervals which do not correspond to the abbreviations.

Melodic

1 P5	2 M3	3 M3	4 m6	5 m3	6 M3
7 m3	8 M2	9 M2	10 T	11 m7	12 P5

Harmonic

1 m3	2 T	3 M6	4 m2	5 P5	6 M6	7 M7	8 T

Octave

The last interval to be considered is the octave, P8. It is twelve half steps above or below the RP. The distance on the staff is large and the pattern of the octave in notation is not clear. It lies four lines and a space above or below an RP on a line, and four spaces and a line above or below an RP on a space.

It may seem unusual that the octave should be discussed as an interval; in harmonic contexts it is usually equated with the unison, or merely a doubling or reinforcing of a particular tone. But melodically the P8 is a powerful interval, implying great strength and distance.

Because the P8 is so distinctive, exercises devoted to this interval will be omitted and we shall proceed directly to exercises involving all intervals.

Tape 8-8___Tonal Memory

Try to sing all seven tones in each group heard.

Exercise 8-3   Visual Recognition: Intervals

Set metronome at 120, four pulses per interval. If this exercise is not easy by now, review earlier units.

Exercise 8-4   Intonation: Octave

Tape 8-9____Imitation with Notation: Review of Intervals

Listen as the tape plays the notes in each measure.
Sing when the tape repeats the measure.

Tape 8-10____Anticipation: Review of Intervals

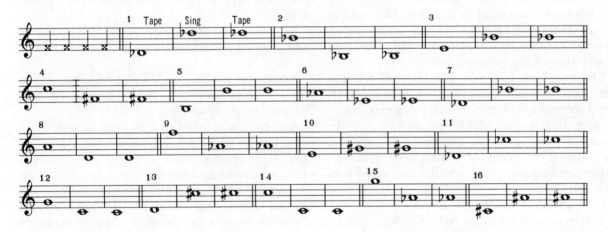

CONFERENCE: Practice Schedule

Ear training requires daily practice. Sporadic efforts will produce minimal results; therefore, schedule ear training study into your daily routine as you do practice time on your instrument or voice. Progress is invariably gradual, often imperceptible, but this is how musicianship evolves.

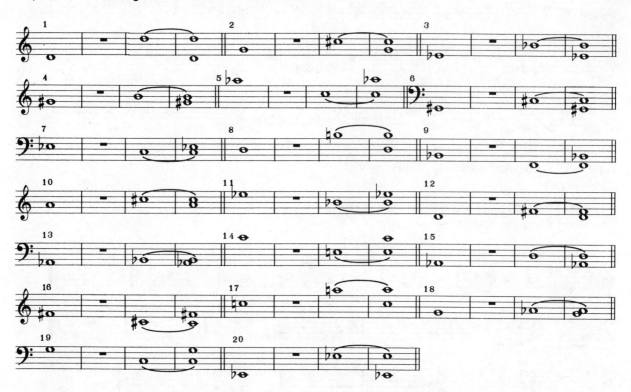

CONFERENCE: Interval Categories

The introduction and discussion of basic intervals has been completed in this unit. Here and in former units listening techniques were recommended. It might be useful to summarize and take an overview of the concepts evolved.

You may have observed that intervals fall into three categories: open, harmonious, and dissonant. Aural recognition of one of these categories should be your first step in identifying an interval, the second step being specific identification—whether the interval is major or minor, for example. Before reading on, recall which intervals fit into each category:

1. open intervals: P4, P5, P8;
2. harmonious intervals: M3, m3, M6, m6;
3. dissonant intervals: M2, m2, M7, m7, T.

It was pointed out that timbre can trick the ear into inverting intervals because of overtones, range, or both.

Also, the open qualities of the P4 and P5 can be confusing even though there is a whole tone difference.

Remember too that the M7 and the tritone (A4 or d5) are often mistaken aurally because of their "leading tone" qualities.

Recognition of intervals is imperative, a skill that must not be delayed beyond this unit. All future aural experiences depend on these building blocks of melodic and harmonic structures. In future units the variety and combination of melodic intervals become increasingly complex. In harmony the changes are even more dramatic. Basic intervals are compounded into new triads and chords which will eventually contain four to seven tones (Book 2).

Tape 8-12____Aural Recognition: Intervals

a. Ascending melodic intervals. Lower note given. Write second note.

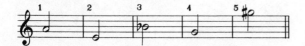

b. Harmonic intervals. Lower note given.

c. Descending melodic intervals. Upper note given.

d. Harmonic intervals. Upper note given.

Tape 8-13____Error Correction: Review of Intervals

Mark an X on those intervals which do not correspond to the abbreviations below.

Melodic
1 P5 2 T 3 m3 4 M6 5 P8 6 M2 7 P8
8 T 9 P5 10 M7

Harmonic
1 T 2 P5 3 m7 4 m6 5 m3 6 M7 7 M3
8 P5 9 P8 10 P4

CONFERENCE: More than One RP

As your inner ear begins to develop, you will find that improvement is being manifested not only in one skill but in many: sight singing, interval identification, intonation, dictation. Tonal memory will also improve, and this skill should be used to good advantage. Gradually, try to keep more than one RP in the inner ear. Often, at the beginning of a melody, you can take not only the tonic pitch as a RP but also the dominant. Sometimes you may be able to keep in your tonal memory the three tones of the tonic triad.

By having more than one RP you can discover other techniques of locating pitches. Your skill with anticipation may produce a useful RP before that tone has been sounded.

The F-sharp above may be located as the lower neighbor tone to the anticipated G. This is more reliable than trying to hear the tritone C to F-sharp.

Look for all the clues you can uncover to make your performance and hearing more efficient and accurate.

In the Rehearsed Melodies, tones in parentheses are to be "heard" as RPs.

HARMONY

Dominant Seventh Chord

The *dominant seventh chord*, V7, consisting of a root, M3, P5, and m7, is a common elaboration or extension of the dominant triad. Another name for the V7 is *major-minor chord* (Mm), so called because the triad is major and the seventh above the root is minor.*

The V7 is generally considered a dissonant chord which requires resolution to the tonic. Notice that the V7 includes a tritone formed by the *third* of the chord (the leading tone of the tonic scale) and the *seventh* (the subdominant degree of the tonic). In resolving the tritone, the tendency of each pitch is to move in the direction described earlier in this unit.

When singing the V7 chord, hear the sonority of the basic triad before attempting the entire four-note chord.

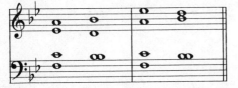

*Other kinds of seventh chords will be studied in the second year of ear training.

125

Exercise 8-5   Fusing: Dominant Seventh Chord

Play the seventh chord shown in measure one. Sing the series of pitches in measure two, in tune, repeating the Mm chord as a drone as often as necessary.

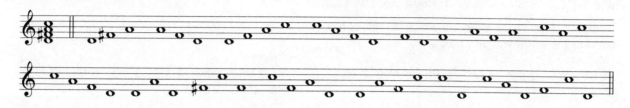

Exercise 8-6   Listening: Dominant Seventh Chord

In a. (below), the seventh is in the top voice. In b. and c. the seventh is shifted to other voices. Practice hearing these root-position major-minor chords in all voicings and ranges. Write other examples that can be played or sung in class.

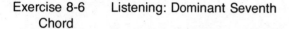

Tape 8-14____Aural Recognition: Chords

Eight chords will be heard on this tape. Indicate the type that is played: M, m, or V7. In the V7 the seventh will always be heard in the highest part.

1   2   3   4
5   6   7   8

Tape 8-15____Aural Recognition: Review of Chords

Major, minor, and V7 chords will be played on this tape, but the seventh will not always be heard in the highest voice. Therefore, listen carefully for the fuller dissonant sonority of the four-note dominant seventh chord as compared to the leaner-sounding triad.

1   2   3   4
5   6   7   8

Sometimes the seventh of the V7 appears as a passing tone in the melody. In such cases it is difficult or impossible to say whether the chord is V7 or V.

Tape 8-16____Aural Recognition: Harmony—
    Dominant-Seventh Chord

Three familiar songs will be sung accompanied by
guitar and cello. Write the progression using roman
numerals.

"Skip to My Lou"

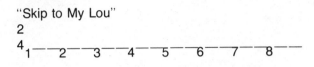

"Long, Long Ago"

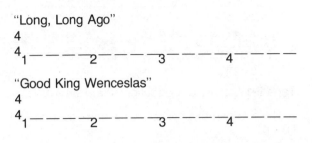

"Good King Wenceslas"

Exercise 8-7   Listening: Harmony

The melody printed below with its three optional
bass lines is an example of the process discussed in
the Unit 7 Conference (p. **107**), the transition of a bass
part from a simple harmonic function to a more in-
dependent, polyphonic role. Hear the melody with
each bass line in the inner ear before performing.

Fill in the chords implied by the bass lines.

Tape 8-17____Error Correction: Two-Part Music

The two-part example below is one you learned in Unit 5.

Review hearing the parts in the inner ear, separately and fused, before playing the tape.

Mark an X where errors appear. Identify the precise mistakes on later listenings.

Haydn, *Lord Nelson Mass "Credo"*

Exercise 8-8   Scanning

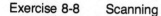

REHEARSED RHYTHM

Perform the following exercises at the speeds given.

REHEARSED MELODIES

Shield

ENSEMBLES

Praetorius

Sweelinck

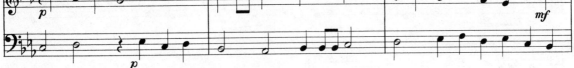

Victoria

© Copyright, Editions Salabert, Paris.
Used by permission of the publisher.

DICTATION

Tape 8-18____Rhythm

A.

Melody

B.

For additional practice in dictation replay Tape 8-2.

C.

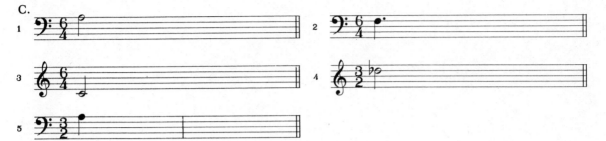

Tape 8-19____Two-Part Music

Listen to this tape several times before writing. Remember to hear in two directions at the same time— horizontally and vertically.

Tape 8-20____Harmony

Write the soprano and bass parts and the symbols for the chords.

UNIT 9

RHYTHM

Level 6

Just as Level 4 was derived from Level 2, Level 6 is derived from Level 3 by subdividing each of the divisions of a compound meter.

Level 1 (BD)

Level 3 (division)

Level 6 (subdivision)

Note that while the various levels of simple division are all reached by dividing by 2, the levels of compound division are not all reached by dividing by 3; the compound series shifts to division by 2. Level 3 divides to become Level 6, not Level 9.

Simple Division   Compound Division

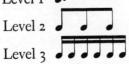

Level 1

Level 2

Level 3

Level 1

Level 2

Level 3

Exercise 9-1   Notation: Rhythm

♪.	♩.	𝅗𝅥.	
			1 + 1 + 1 + 1 + 1 + 1
			2 + 1 + 1 + 1 + 1
			1 + 2 + 1 + 1 + 1
			1 + 1 + 2 + 1 + 1
			1 + 1 + 1 + 2 + 1
			1 + 1 + 1 + 1 + 2 +
			2 + 2 + 1 + 1
			1 + 2 + 2 + 1
			1 + 1 + 2 + 2
			1 + 2 + 1 + 2
			2 + 2 + 2
			1 + 2 + 3
			2 + 1 + 3
			1 + 3 + 2
			2 + 3 + 1
			3 + 2 + 1
			3 + 1 + 2
			3 + 3
			3 + 1 + 1 + 1
			4 + 1 + 1
			4 + 2
			1 + 1 + 4
			2 + 4
			5 + 1
			1 + 5
			1 + 4 + 1
			6

Here are the various possibilities of compound subdivision (Level 6). Complete the notation.

Not all of the above rhythms are used with equal frequency. Many of them are quite difficult to perform accurately; practice at Levels 1 and 3 will help one gain fluency and confidence.

Exercise 9-2   Rhythm: Ratios

The following exercises will offer practice in working with some of the more common Level 6 rhythms. If you are familiar with these rhythms try writing your own exercises using some of the less familiar ones.

Tape 9-1_____Imitation with Notation: Rhythm—
    Level 6

In the second bar imitate rhythm that was played
in the first bar.

Tape 9-2___Error Correction: Rhythm—
Level 6

Mark an X over rhythms that are not notated as performed on the tape.

INTERVALS

Tape 9-3___Tonal Memory: Review of Intervals

A pattern of eight pitches will be heard. Repeat what you hear before the tape replays the series so you can check accuracy.

Exercise 9-3   Visual Recognition: Review of Intervals

With the metronome set at 112 identify each interval within four pulses.

Exercise 9-4   Intonation: Multiple RPs

Practice the exercise playing the drone as often as necessary to check the intonation between the drone and the tone you are singing. Then sing the exercise, playing the drone as *little* as possible, keeping this pitch in your inner ear. As the exercise progresses other tones will occur prominently and frequently enough to stick in your tonal memory, becoming auxiliary RPs. Strive to reach the point where you have many RPs stored in your tonal memory bank.

You should have these RPs well established in your inner ear when this exercise is completed.

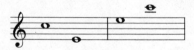

CONFERENCE: Inversion of Intervals

A given harmonic interval may be inverted by moving the upper tone down an octave or by moving the lower tone up an octave.

Note the relationship of these sonorities. Being able to hear and sing the inversion of intervals can be useful in singing very wide intervals and in learning to change octaves when a melody moves beyond your vocal range.

Inversions of intervals are generally fairly easy to recognize on the staff. Those same intervals can be elusive to the ear, particularly when descending.

An inverted interval should be heard in these ways:

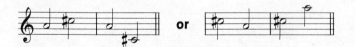

If the procedure is difficult, try this intermediate exercise until the inner ear can hear inversions.

This exercise emphasizes the octave relationship within the inverted interval. Ultimately, the goal is to hear the pivotal relationship of the RP to the inverted pitches.

Tape 9-4____Imitation with Notation: Review of Intervals

Tape 9-5____Anticipation: Review of Intervals

Tape 9-6____Aural Recognition: Review of Intervals

Melodic					Harmonic				
1	2	3	4	5	1	2	3	4	5
6	7	8	9	10	6	7	8	9	10

Tape 9-7____Error Correction: Melody

Mark an X over the measures where errors are found. Identify the exact error in later hearings.

Sing and hear these exercises in major and minor, interchanging A-natural and A-flat in the V chord in minor. In some modes the V chord is minor instead of major.

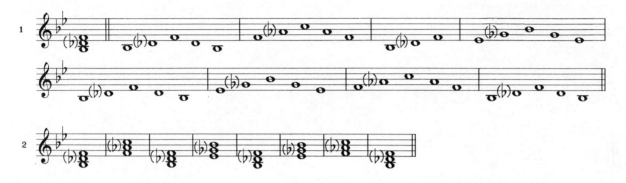

HARMONY

First Inversion of Chords

A chord need not always have its root in the lowest part. The *third*, *fifth*, or *seventh* may appear as the bass note. The most common of these inversions is the *first inversion* ($^6_3$ or 6) in which the third of the chord is found in the bass.

Aurally, a triad in first inversion will sound less solid than the firmer sonority of the triad in root position.

Tape 9-8____Listening: Triads in Root Position and First Inversion

Six major and six minor triads, first in root position, then in first inversion, will be played. Notice the difference in the sonority.

Tape 9-10____Listening: Harmony—First Inversion

On first hearing, the melody will be accompanied by a bass line only. The second time it will be fully harmonized.

Listen for the quality, inversion, and function of the harmony.

Tape 9-9____Aural Recognition: Triads in Root Position and First Inversion

Identify the following triads. Use M or m for major and minor in root position, M^6_3 or m^6_3 for first inversion.

1	2	3	4	5	6
7	8	9	10	11	12

V⁶ I I⁶ V V   V   V⁶ I V I⁶ IV V   V⁶ I I⁶ IV IV⁶ I IV I IV⁶

I I⁶ I V I

Tape 9-11___Anticipation: Harmony

In these progressions use the rest in the lower parts to anticipate the following chord. These are more difficult exercises which may need repetition but are well worth the effort. Eventually you should be able to anticipate the quality and function of the I, IV, and V chords as well as hear the horizontal role of the individual parts.

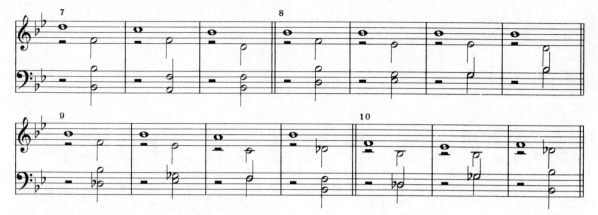

Tape 9-12____Error Correction: Harmony

In these brief progressions there are one or more errors: either the quality, inversion, or function will be wrong. Mark the places where errors appear and, if possible, correct the notation.

Tape 9-13____Two-Part Music

Three intervals will be played. Identify the relative action between the first and second and second and third by writing P, S, C, or O.

1__ __ 2__ __ 3__ __ 4__ __ 5__ __ 6__ __ 7__ __ 8__ __ 9__ __ 10__ __

Tape 9-14____Error Correction: Two-Part Music

The two-part example shown below was one learned in Unit 3.

Review it in the inner ear before you play this tape.

Mark an X where errors occur, then identify the mistakes on subsequent hearings.

Exercise 9-6   Scanning

REHEARSED MELODIES

Try to count at level 6 where indicated

Mexico

Polish Melody

English Melody

ENSEMBLES

Handel

* The interval here is actually a diminished seventh, but you can
sing this easily if you hear the B as a half step below your C (RP).

SIGHT-READING

1

2

Handel, *Judas Maccabaeus*

3

English Folksong

4

Langsam ♩ = 88

Bruckner, *Tantum Ergo*

5

♩. = 96

Flemish Folksong

MORE DIFFICULT

Vivaldi, *Lauda Jerusalem*

DICTATION

Tape 9-15_____Rhythm

Melody

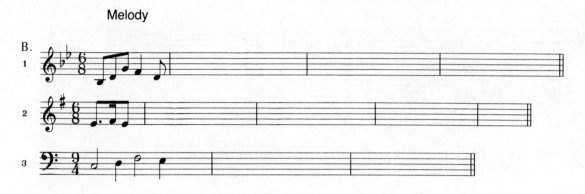

For additional dictation practice replay Tape 9-3.
Starting notes given below.

Tape 9-16____Two-Part Music

Tape 9-17____Harmony

A short melody will be harmonized in three different ways. Complete the melody, then write the bass notes and roman numerals under each chord; write "6" to indicate first inversion.

Additional dictation.

B.

A : i

C.

B♭ :I

D.

G♭ :I

UNIT 10

INTERVALS

Harmonic Minor Scale

The *harmonic minor* scale is readily identified because of the augmented second, A2, in the second tetrachord.

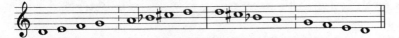

The raised seventh degree affords a leading tone in the scale, and a major triad for the dominant chord.

Observe too that this scale has three half steps, between 2 and 3, 5 and 6, and 7 and 8.

Tape 10-1____Tonal Memory

Five melodies will be heard. After each is played, sing, then listen as the tape plays back the phrase.

Exercise 10-1   Visual Recognition: Augmented Second

Set the metronome at 80. Allow four pulses to decide each interval. Notice the clefs on the first two staves and the key signatures on the third and fourth.

Exercise 10-2   Intonation: Harmonic Minor Scale

If this exercise seems boring, you are not practicing it correctly! Keep as many RPs as possible in your tonal memory.

These RPs should be firmly retained in your inner ear.

Tape 10-2____Imitation with Notation: Review of
   Intervals

An interval will be played. Repeat it immediately in tempo.

Tape 10-3_____Imitation with Notation: Inversion of
   Intervals

The tape plays the interval in measure one; repeat
its inversion as shown in the next measure.

Tape 10-4_____Anticipation: Review of Intervals

Tape 10-5_____Aural Recognition: Review of Intervals

Write the symbol for the interval after each number.

Melodic					Harmonic				
1	2	3	4	5	1	2	3	4	5
6	7	8	9	10	6	7	8	9	10

Tape 10-6_____Error Correction: Melody

Mark an X over any measure where an error is
heard. Try to identify the errors.

First Inversion of the Dominant Seventh Chord

In the first inversion of the dominant-seventh chord, V_5^6, the leading tone in the bass is quite prominent. The tritone and the m7 (or M2) dissonance of the root to the seventh will also be heard in the *quality* of the sonority. Since the V_5^6 is a four-note chord, it will be thicker sounding than the V triad; however, the V_5^6 will not be as strong a sonority as the V7 in root position.

Tape 10-7_____Listening with Notation: V_5^6

Notice the changes in sonority that result when different chord tones are placed in the soprano part.

Each example will be performed twice: first in major, then in minor.

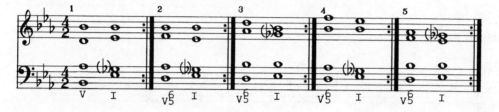

Exercise 10-3   Fusing: V_5^6

Play the drone chord as many times as necessary while singing this exercise. Tune each tone carefully. After the chord is thoroughly assimilated by the inner ear try singing it at faster and faster tempi.

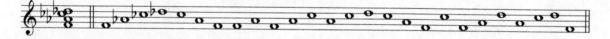

Tape 10-8_____Aural Recognition: Harmony

This tape will test your ability to differentiate between the V triad in root position ($_3^5$) and the first inversion (6), and the four-note V7 and V_5^6. Write the symbols after the numbers. You will hear a V or V7 (root position or first inversion) followed by a I. Identify the V.

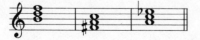

1   2   3   4   5
6   7   8

vii° Chord

When a triad is built on the seventh degree of the scale—a half step below the tonic—a *diminished triad* results, so named because of the d5. The triad itself consists of two minor thirds.

Aurally, it can be difficult to distinguish between the V7 and vii°. Not only are they similar in *function,* but the *qualities* of their sonorities are extremely similar. Of course, the primary thing to listen for is the difference in thickness between the three-note vii° and the four-note V7. This subtle quality difference can be elusive when the dominant seventh chord is in first inversion (V$^6_5$) because both chords have a common bass note and a tritone between the fourth and seventh degrees of the scale.

When the vii° triad is in first inversion there is little change in the quality due to the uniformity of its intervallic structure—two minor thirds. In Unit 11 we shall see that it is fairly easy to confuse the vii°6 with the second inversion of the dominant seventh chord (V$^4_3$) since both have a common bass note. Do not be too concerned if you occasionally mistake vii° for an inversion of V7.

Tape 10-9____Listening with Notation: vii° Triad

Listen while watching the notation. Later, look away and replay the tape sensing the quality, inversion, and function of each chord.

Exercise 10-4   Fusing: Diminished Triad

Play the drone chord in measure one. Sing the exercise as slowly as you wish, always tuning each note carefully. The diminished triad is given here in its root position, first inversion, and as a four-note chord.

When you can sing each exercise forward, try singing in retrograde.

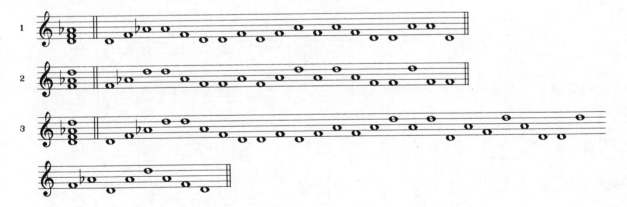

Tape 10-10____Aural Recognition: Harmony

You will hear a V-type chord resolving to the I. Differentiate the vii° and vii°6, the V, V7, and V$^6_5$.

1	2	3	4	5
6	7	8		

Exercise 10-5   Fusing

This exercise is similar to the one introduced in Unit 9. Its purpose is to help make the transition from horizontal to vertical hearing. Notice the first inversions and diminished triads.

Before moving on to No. 2 below, learn No. 1 thoroughly or the inner ear will not be able to hear the tones simultaneously.

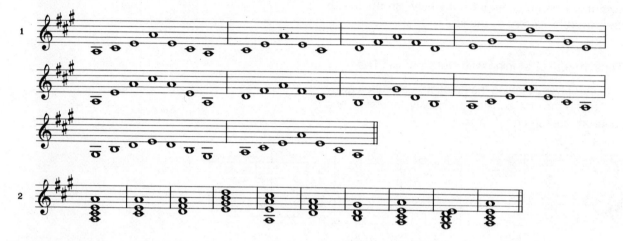

Exercise 10-6   Visual Recognition: Chords

Set the metronome at 72 and allow six pulses to identify each chord.

Exercise 10-7   Fusing: Function

This melody with its three versions of a bass line shows the transition of a bass line from its simplest harmonic form to a more contrapuntal line which complements the top voice.

Practice this exercise using the same procedures as before:

1. Practice both parts until they can be heard melodically.

2. Fuse the two parts until each harmonic interval is heard.

3. Lastly, hear as written.

The piano is not your friend if you want to develop the inner ear; therefore, resist the temptation to go to the keyboard before you hear the piece mentally.

Tape 10-11   Anticipation: Harmony

While the RP is sounding at the beginning of each measure, anticipate the harmony that follows.

Tape 10-12   Error Correction: Harmony

Correct errors in quality, inversion, or function.

g: I V$^6_5$ I I6   I vii6 V7 I   I vii° V7 I   I6 V7 I V   I V6 V7 I

Tape 10-13   Error Correction: Two-Part Music

This two-part exercise appeared in Unit 6. Review it
in your inner ear before playing the tape. When errors
occur, mark an X. During later hearings correct the
errors.

Exercise 10-8   Scanning

REHEARSED RHYTHM

The introduction of dynamics and accents into these exercises presents new problems. Intone the exercises at the tempos recommended. The faster the tempo, the more the eye should take in complete measures and sweep ahead of the moment of the performance.

REHEARSED MELODIES

ENSEMBLES

Describe the relationship of the parts in this ensemble.

SIGHT-READING

MORE DIFFICULT

DICTATION

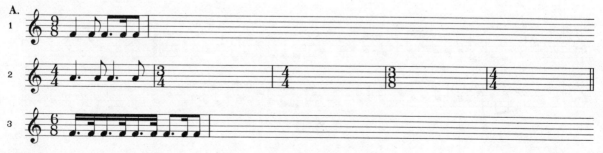

Melody

For additional dictation practice replay Tape 10-1.
Starting pitches are given below.

Tape 10-15____Two-Part Music

Tape 10-16___Harmony

A melody in e minor will be performed with first
inversions of triads and the dominant seventh chord.
The I⁶₄ and root position chords are also used.

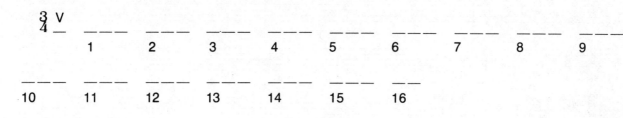

Tape 10-17___Harmony

Complete the soprano and bass parts. Write roman
numerals below each new chord.

170

UNIT 11

RHYTHM

Level 8

By now the concept of rhythmic level should be familiar. Recall how the charts showing all of the rhythmic possibilities at each level have grown longer and longer (compare the charts on pages 5 , 41 , 60 , and 138). The number of possible rhythmic ratios for Level 8 is so large that it is impractical to write out the complete list. However, you should be able to visualize the list. It would start like this:

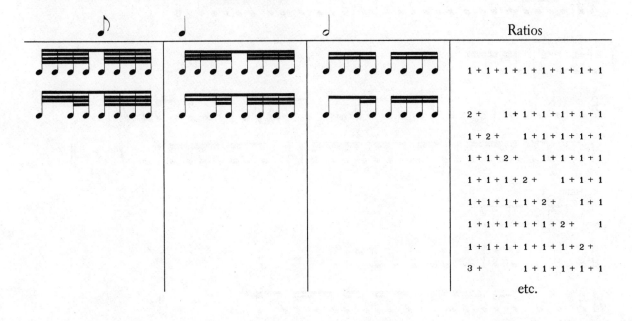

♪	♩	𝅗𝅥	Ratios
			1 + 1 + 1 + 1 + 1 + 1 + 1 + 1
			2 + 1 + 1 + 1 + 1 + 1 + 1
			1 + 2 + 1 + 1 + 1 + 1 + 1
			1 + 1 + 2 + 1 + 1 + 1 + 1
			1 + 1 + 1 + 2 + 1 + 1 + 1
			1 + 1 + 1 + 1 + 2 + 1 + 1
			1 + 1 + 1 + 1 + 1 + 2 + 1
			1 + 1 + 1 + 1 + 1 + 1 + 2 +
			3 + 1 + 1 + 1 + 1 + 1
			etc.

Exercise 11-1   Rhythm: Level 8

Of the many possible rhythms available at Level 8, several are used more commonly than others and deserve particular attention. If these rhythms give you trouble they may be practiced at Level 4.

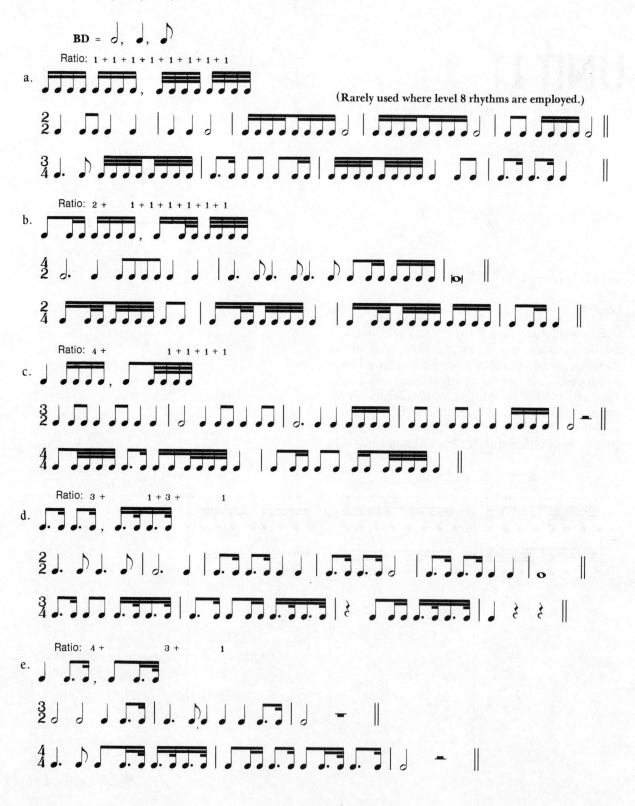

(Rarely used where level 8 rhythms are employed.)

Ratio: 6 +   1 + 1

Tape 11-1___Error Correction: Rhythm

The rhythms heard and those you see on the page will not always match. Mark where errors occur and write in the corrections.

MODES

Mixolydian

A scale will be played on Tape 11-2, beginning on the note f′, which will require accidentals to make it match what is heard.

1. Mark the places where the half steps appear.
2. Write the key signature after the clef.
3. Sing the scale with the tape, then without.

Tape 11-2___Listening: Mixolydian Mode

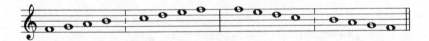

The scale you have just heard, written, and sung is called the Mixolydian. It is sometimes mistaken for major because of the half step between 3 and 4 in the first tetrachord; however, the half step between 6 and 7 lends this scale a quality which seems to vacillate between major and minor.

CONFERENCE: Tonal Memory

The number of pitches to be sung in this unit's tonal memory exercises will be increased from eight to ten.

By adding more pitches to be retained in the inner ear two objectives should be achieved: (1) you will begin thinking of and memorizing music in broader terms—from melodic motives to phrases, to periods, to sections and so on; (2) tonal memory should converge with melodic dictation, thereby allowing you to retain and write down longer and longer melodies.

Exercise 11-2   Intonation: Mixolydian Mode,
     Review

Exercise 11-3   Visual Recognition: Mixolydian
     Mode

1. Choose any Rehearsed Melody in this unit, set
the metronome at a moderate speed (80–92), and
allow four pulses to name each successive interval.

2. Select another Rehearsed Melody and determine if it is in Mixolydian or not, and list the reasons
for your conclusion.

Tape 11-3____Tonal Memory

Listen for the series, sing, then listen for the replay to check accuracy. It is suggested that these
tonal-memory tapes be repeated until all the exercises can be sung correctly.

INTERVALS

Exercise 11-4   Inversion of Intervals

Play the RP, then sing the exercise as written. In the beginning it is not necessary to maintain a tempo, but eventually try to sing the inversions at faster and faster metronome settings. If an inversion is difficult to sing at one of the quicker speeds, isolate it and practice until the inner ear hears the intervals. Once again, remember that the vocal cords can only respond to what the mind and inner ear have already heard. Step one is aural comprehension; step two is singing.

A variation of the Inversion of Intervals exercise introduced in Unit 9 is *Mirror Inversion.* In this exercise the same interval is sung in *both* directions.

Exercise 11-5   Mirror Inversion of Intervals

In Unit 9, inversion of intervals at the octave was discussed. In that type of inversion the upper tone is transposed down an octave or the lower tone is transposed up an octave.

In mirror inversion the ascent or descent is merely reversed by the same distance, i.e., an ascending P4 becomes a descending P4. This technique is found frequently in contemporary music. Singing mirror inversions requires thought. In a complex passage you may not be able to keep extended RPs, in which case you must rely on your ability to hear intervals abstractly (without reference to a tonal center).

Practice the following series of expanding mirror inversions.

When you have learned to do this exercise make up more challenging drills for yourself by singing any three- or four-note pattern and then singing its mirror inversion.

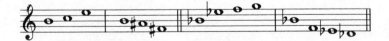

Tape 11-4_____Anticipation: Review of Intervals

Tape 11-5_____Error Correction: Review of Intervals

The intervals shown below may not be the same as those played on the tape. Identify the errors; write the corrections. The first note in melodic intervals and the bottom note in harmonic intervals will always be correct.

Tape 11-6_____Error Correction: Melody

First mark, later identify measures where wrong rhythms and pitches occur in the performance.

Tape 11-7_____Error Correction: Two-Part Music

The ensemble shown here was printed in Unit 6. If you learned it previously, review the ensemble before playing the tape. If it was not studied, practice the individual parts and fuse until it can be heard in the inner ear.

When playing the tape, identify errors and make notations on the staff.

176

HARMONY

Second Inversion of the Triad

A *second inversion*, $^6_4$, of a chord occurs when the fifth is placed in the bass. The sonority of this chord makes it particularly useful in cadences. For example, just as the dominant seventh chord implies resolution to the tonic that follows, the sonority of the I^6_4 implies the following *two* chords—the dominant and tonic.

A I^6_4 produces a sense of anticipation. Its unique sonority and function help to identify this second inversion.

In its isolated state the second inversion is the weakest sonority of the three forms (root, $^6_3$, $^6_4$) of a major or minor triad. This chord has an unstable quality, like a dissonance needing resolution.

Tape 11-8____Listening with Notation: Second Inversion

a. Five isolated second-inversion major and minor triads will be heard.

b. A major chord in root position, first inversion, and second inversion will be played. A minor chord in the same order will follow.

c. These progressions will be heard:

1. I I$^6_4$ V I
2. i i$^6_4$ V i
3. I I6 IV I$^6_4$ V7 I
4. i i6 iv i$^6_4$ V7 i

Exercise 11-6   Fusing: Second Inversion of the Triad

Repeat the drone frequently as this exercise is sung. Sing with higher and higher metronome settings.

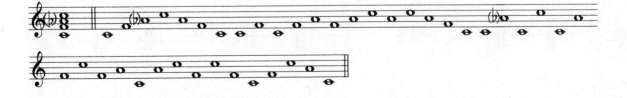

Second Inversion of the Dominant Seventh Chord

A *second inversion* of a dominant seventh, V_3^4, occurs when the fifth is written in the bass. The V_3^4 is usually a passing chord, connecting the preceding and the following chords.

I6 V_3^4 I

A V_3^4 sonority is not as strong as the V7 or V_5^6 but the *quality* and gravitation of the dominant seventh to the tonic is still strong. Often the *inversion* and the *function* of the bass note of the V_3^4, its proximity and movement to the tonic (I) or third degree of the scale (I6), is a clue to its presence in a progression. The V_3^4 is often confused with the vii°6, but the latter has a thinner sonority.

Tape 11-9____Listening with Notation: V_3^4

a. Five V_3^4 chords in diverse keys will be played.

b. A dominant seventh chord will be heard in root position—V7, first inversion—V_5^6, and V_3^4.

c. The following progressions will be played.

1. I V_3^4 I6 IV V_3^4 I
2. i V_3^4 i6 iv V_3^4 i

Exercise 11-7   Fusing: Second Inversion of the Dominant Seventh Chord

Play the drone chord at the beginning and whenever it is needed to maintain good intonation. Tune every note carefully. Set the metronome at different speeds once you are confident of the inversion.

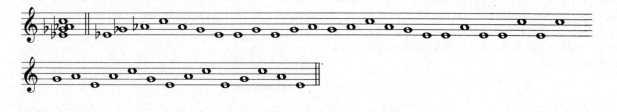

Exercise 11-8   Fusing: Function

Sing No. 1 until all chords can be sung with ease and with no pauses between measures. In the process keep thinking: this exercise is a melodic realization of a harmonic progression. Each chord should eventually be heard as an instantaneous experience as in No. 2. It might prove useful to sing the bass note of each chord in No. 2 as one of the steps in making the transition from horizontal to vertical sonorities.

Sing in major and minor.

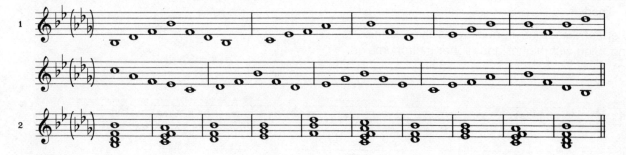

Abstract chords, out of harmonic context, will be played. Write the symbol for each after the numbers. The chords included are the following:

1. M M$_3^6$ $_4^6$
2. m m$_3^6$ m$_4^6$
3. vii° vii° 6
4. V7 V$_5^6$ V$_3^4$

1. Identify the chord quality and inversion.

1	2	3	4	5
6	7	8	9	10
11	12	13	14	15
16	17	18	19	20

2. Replay the tape and identify the chord tone that appears in the soprano.

1	2	3	4	5
6	7	8	9	10
11	12	13	14	15
16	17	18	19	20

Exercise 11-9   Visual Recognition: Chords

Set the metronome at 72 and allow five pulses for naming each chord. Name quality and inversion.

Tape 11-11_____Anticipation: Harmony

When the RP is sounded at the beginning of each measure, anticipate the chord that follows.

Study and fuse these examples. Locate and correct errors.

Fermata

The *fermata* (plural: *fermate*) is traditionally used at points of special significance in musical works. Suspension of the pulse calls attention to the event, whether it is the sustaining of a tone or chord, or a prolonged silence. In the middle of a work a fermata often creates a sense of anticipation of what is to come. In any case, the approach to, duration of, and resumption of the music following a fermata invariably requires good taste and judgment.

Exercise 11-10   Scanning

REHEARSED MELODIES

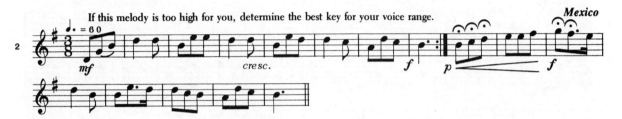

If this melody is too high for you, determine the best key for your voice range.

Mexico

English Folksong

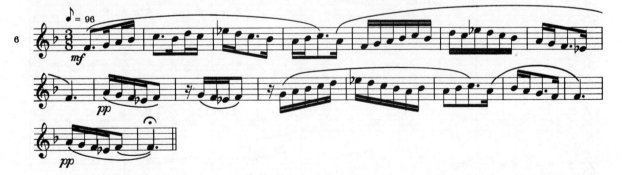

Better look over the rhythm before you begin.

Holst, *The Coming of Christ*

© Copyright by G. Schirmer, Inc., New York
Used by permission of the publisher

Australian Folksong

Moderato (♪ = 108)

Mendelssohn

ENSEMBLES

SIGHT-READING

183

MORE DIFFICULT

DICTATION

Tape 11-13_____Rhythm

Melody

Tape 11-14____Two-Part Music

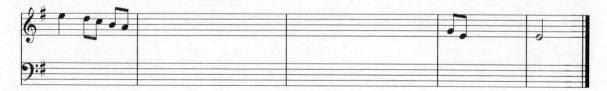

Tape 11-15____Harmony

What are the melodic and harmonic elements that lend this folksong its modal quality? Can you point out the subtle events at cadences which add color and charm to this piece?

Fill in the chord symbols where the chords change in each measure.

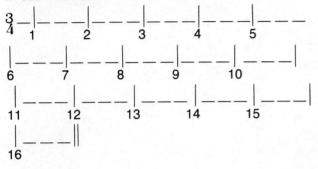

Tape 11-16   Harmony

Write the soprano and bass parts and the chord symbols.

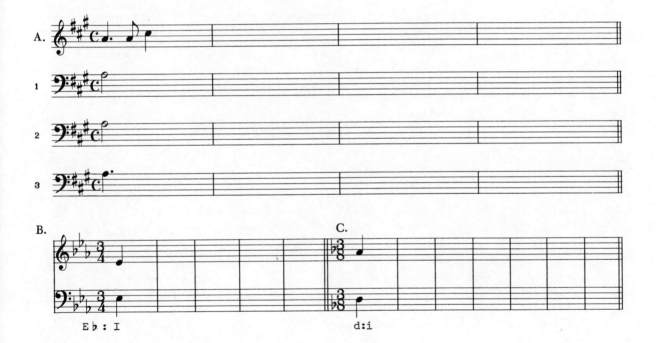

UNIT 12

HARMONY

Third Inversion of the Dominant Seventh Chord

The *third inversion* of a dominant seventh chord, V_2^4, occurs when the seventh is written in the bass. In most cases the V_2^4 resolves in the manner shown below—the seventh moving downward to a major or minor first-inversion tonic triad.

Aurally, the V_2^4 is the most dissonant of the inversions of the V7 chord and, consequently, one of the easier chords to recognize. There is a special sonority that characterizes the V_2^4: the downward harmonic tension of the bass resolving to a tonic chord. When the distance between the bass and the upper voices is great, the sonority of V_2^4 may resemble a major triad with a "wrong" bass note.

Tape 12-1____Listening with Notation: V_2^4

a. Five abstract V_2^4 chords will be played.
b. You will hear V7, V_5^6, V_3^4, and V_2^4 in succession. Listen for the differences in the sonorities.
c. The following progressions will be heard:

1. I V_2^4 I6
2. i V_2^4 i6
3. I I6 IV I_4^6 V7 V_2^4 I6 V_3^4 I
4. i iv i_4^6 V_2^4 i6 V7 i

Exercise 12-1   Fusing: V$^4_2$

Repeat the drone chord in measure one as many times as necessary to maintain intonation.

Sing "out of tempo" until the V$^4_2$ has been mastered, then try this exercise at different speeds with a metronome.

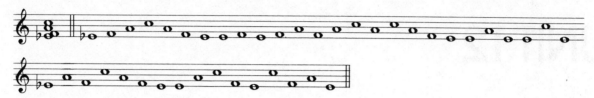

Exercise 12-2   Fusing: Function

Sing No. 1 until the transition from one chord to another is smooth. While singing the melodic version (1) be thinking vertical, instantaneous chords.

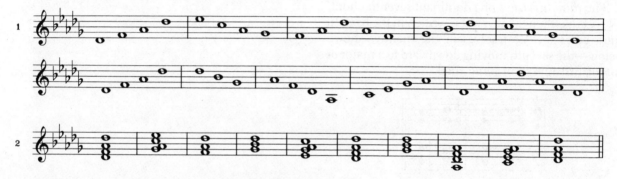

Tape 12-2____Aural Recognition: Review of Chords

Twenty isolated chords will be played. Write their symbols after the numbers. Use M, m, V7, 6, $^4_2$, and so forth.

1	2	3	4	5
6	7	8	9	10
11	12	13	14	15
16	17	18	19	20

190

Exercise 12-3   Visual Recognition of Chords

Set your metronome at 76. Allow four pulses for
each identification.

Tape 12-3____Anticipation: Harmony

Anticipate the chords that follow the RPs.

These brief progressions are to be studied, fused, and heard mentally before the tape is played. Circle and correct the errors in quality, inversion, or function.

CONFERENCE: Review of Listening Experiences in Harmony

Now that the third inversion of the dominant seventh chord has been introduced, let us summarize what has been covered in harmonic listening experiences.

Quality. There are *three* qualities of triads that you should be able to identify: *major, minor,* and *diminished.* Discovering the quality of a chord should be your first objective and precedes concern with identifying inversion and function.

The quality of the *dominant seventh chord* is major, but the addition of the seventh to the basic triad lends this chord a unique sonority. Therefore, this four-tone chord is a separate aural experience.

The philosophy of this textbook has been that each chord is an aural experience that must be learned so that its sonority is recognized immediately. When the qualities and inversions studied so far are totaled, you should be distinguishing *thirteen* chords: M, $^6_3$, $^6_4$; m, $^6_3$, $^6_4$, d, $^6_3$, $^6_4$; V7, $^6_5$, $^4_3$, $^4_2$.

Root Position. This is the strongest sonority of a triad or chord; however, because of the function of chords within specific keys, even root-position chords have diverse harmonic intensities. For example, the I chord in root position will sound more stable than a IV chord in root position.

First Inversion. Although this inversion is not as strong as a chord in root position, it is still an intense sonority. In harmonic sequences, first inversions have about the same flexibility as root position chords.

Second Inversion. The second inversion is somewhat unstable as a sonority; its tendency is to lead on to the next sonority. As demonstrated in this text, the function of the I$^6_4$ or i$^6_4$ is to prepare for the V or V7 chord at a cadence. The V$^4_3$ often functions as a passing chord.

Third Inversion. The only example of this inversion that was discussed was the V$^4_2$, the most dissonant sonority of all the chords and inversions you have studied. The seventh in the bass of the V$^4_2$ almost always descends to the third of a I or i, forming the I6 or i6.

Function. The particular function of a chord is determined by the context—by its relationship to the tonic. Some theorists classify all diatonic chords into three groups: the tonic, the dominant, and the subdominant. Under this system, chords with a dominant function include V, V7, and vii° and all their inversions. The similarity between these sonorities is so great that it is sometimes difficult to distinguish between them. In the subdominant category there are two chords, the IV and the ii—the ii frequently serving as a substitute for the IV. We will work with the ii later in this book, as well as with the vi, which in deceptive cadences replaces the tonic.

Learning to identify the function of a particular chord is a matter of experience—verbal explanations fall far short in describing these aural phenomena. The only way to recognize the IV is to listen to the sonority in context often enough that the sound becomes familiar. At this time you should be able to recognize the functions of I, V, IV, and vii°, in major and minor.

The difficulty of identifying a particular chord may depend on its context. An observation made earlier about intervals also pertains to harmony: a particular harmony may not be difficult in itself, but because of what preceded it. For this reason, learn to identify all chords and inversions in two ways: as abstract sounds and as sonorities that function in harmonic progressions.

Returning to the question of which chords will be easier or more difficult to hear, it can be said that the difference between *major* and *minor* qualities should be readily distinguishable. The *diminished* quality will be easier to hear as an abstract triad than in context, where it is frequently confused with the *dominant seventh chord*. The sharpness of dissonance and the downward resolution of the V_2^4 is apparent to most students. And the function of the I_4^6 anticipating the dominant is an idiomatic harmonic progression that one soon learns.

One's previous solo and ensemble experiences will have a bearing on one's ability to identify various harmonies. Pianists can imagine harmonies readily because of the nature of their instrument, more so than a singer or a clarinetist. A person who plays a trombone or a cello or who sings bass in a choir can usually hear inversions better than the student who sings or plays a treble part. All these variations in students' natural or acquired skills exist in every ear-training class. It is important that each student evaluate objectively his or her own aural development, then emphasize those areas where deficiencies are found.

MODES

Dorian Mode

Tape 12-5___Dorian Mode

1. On the staff below write the accidentals needed to make the scale consistent with what was heard.
2. Mark the half steps.

3. Write the key signature and sing the scale ascending and descending with and without the tape. Start on new RPs and see if you can sing the Dorian scale accurately.

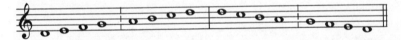

One of the first things you may have noticed when listening to the Dorian mode is that it has a minor quality because of the half step between 2 and 3 in the first tetrachord. In fact, Dorian scales are often mistaken for *natural minor*. The difference in Dorian occurs in the second tetrachord when the half step appears between 6 and 7, *not* 5 and 6, as in natural minor.

Tape 12-6___Tonal Memory

Sing each melodic phrase after it is played on the tape. Listen or sing along when the phrase is repeated.

CONFERENCE: Intonation Studies

The conscientious practicing of intonation exercises is an important step toward developing musicianship. If you have neglected them you have eliminated an indispensable part of your development.

There are two benefits to intonation studies. The first was mentioned in the Unit 2 conference on intonation—gaining awareness and skill in hearing music in tune.

Equally important is that you will become more aware of the changing relationships of intervals in various scales, particularly in the less familiar modes.

Scales, like intervals and chords, are learned experiences which are only acquired through repetition. So do not neglect these exercises!

Exercise 12-4   Intonation: Dorian Mode

In this exercise be particularly careful of the tuning of C-sharp and G-natural.

Also, at this stage in your development of tonal memory you should have every tone of the Dorian scale in the inner ear as an available RP by the time you complete this exercise.

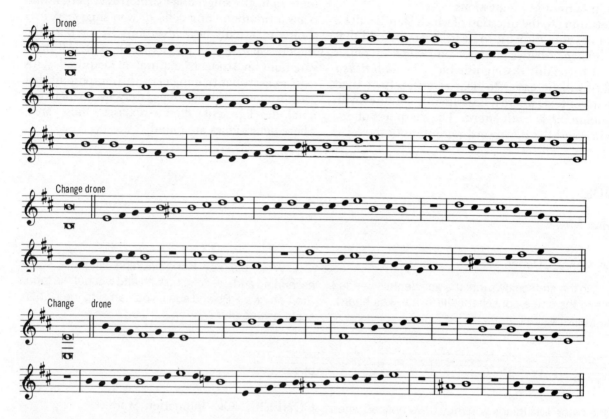

Exercise 12-5   Mirror Inversion of Motives

Sing the original melody first, then invert it. If you have difficulty singing the inversion, write the melody in its mirror-inversion form.

If these exercises seemed easy invent more difficult ones with traps for the eye and ear. Then try them on friends in class.

Ionian and Aeolian Modes

Both modes are very familiar but under different names: the Ionian mode is the same as the *major scale;* and the Aeolian mode is the same as the *natural minor* scale. Since both scales have been covered in previous units the only thing to remember is their modal names.

INTERVALS

Tape 12-7____Anticipation: Review of Intervals and Inversions

This anticipation exercise will be slightly different from those found in earlier units. After the RP, sing the interval *and* its inversion. As before, the tape will then play the correct intervals.

Tape 12-8____Error Correction: Intervals

If the interval played on the tape does not coincide with the one on the staff, circle, then correct the notation. The lower note in melodic intervals and harmonic intervals will always be notated correctly.

Melodic

Harmonic

Tape 12-9____Error Correction: Melody

Listen for the rhythmic and melodic errors in this tape; write in rhythms or pitches heard.

This ensemble was learned in Unit 9. Indicate where errors in pitch and rhythm occur.

RHYTHM

Mixed Levels

Mixed levels of rhythm result when *simple* and *compound* divisions are juxtaposed.

Example 1 below is in $\frac{4}{4}$, a simple meter, but compound-division triplets are present. Example 2 is in $\frac{6}{8}$, a compound meter, but there are simple duplets present.

Two fundamentals worth remembering when performing mixed levels are:
1. The BD does not change, it remains constant.
2. Maintain a steady pulse, and be able to shift between simple and compound division.

Exercise 12-6   Rehearsed Rhythm

Tape 12-11_____Error Correction: Rhythm

Mark those places where there are rhythmic errors,
then correct them.

Tempo Changes

There are two categories of tempo changes:
immediate and *gradual*.

In *immediate* changes you should have a clear
concept of the original tempo and the new tempo.
Practice with and without a metronome until you
are able to recall both tempi at any moment.

Gradual changes of tempo not only call for a clear
concept of both tempos but also an awareness of the
time the composer allowed between them.

Most times it is possible to progress smoothly
through changes of tempo in performances. At other
times it is practical to change speeds on the down-
beats of successive measures. This *terraced* technique is often used with large performing groups
where subtle nuances of tempo within measures are
difficult to communicate.

The rhythmic levels discussed in this book have
an important role in tempo changes and are indispensable in achieving accuracy during transitions.
Levels 1 and 2 will be useful in ritardandos, the
higher levels in accelerandos. Avoid unintentional
crescendos when accelerating, *diminuendos* when
retarding.

Exercise 12-7   Tempo Changes

Exercise 12-8   Rehearsed Rhythm

Exercise 12-9   Scanning

198

REHEARSED MELODIES

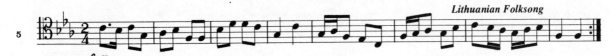

Clap

ENSEMBLES

et in sen - su_____ co - gi -ta - -bit cir-cum spe - cti -
tur et in sen - su co - gi - ta - - bit cir-cum spe -
o - nem De_____ cir - cum spe - cti - o -
- cti - o - nem_____ De - - - i cir - cum spe - cti -
nem De - - - - - - - i.
o - nem De - - - - - - - i.

SIGHT-READING

Lampe

Verdi, *Requiem*

Australian Folksong

MORE DIFFICULT

DICTATION

Tape 12-12_____Rhythm

A.

5 $\frac{6}{8}$ [music notation]

Melody

B.
1
2
3
4
5

For additional practice in dictation replay Tape 12-6.

C.
1   2   3   4
5

Tape 12-13____Two-Part Music

Scarlatti

CONFERENCE: Modal Harmony

The interval structure of the modes determines the qualities of the triads. In Dorian, for instance, the i chord is minor, the IV chord is major, and the v chord is minor. Thus, on particular degrees, we are surprised to hear a quality which differs from the familiar patterns of major and minor keys.

Before moving on to a harmonization of a Dorian melody practice fusing the principal triads. This procedure will definitely help you hear implied harmonies in the folksong that follows.

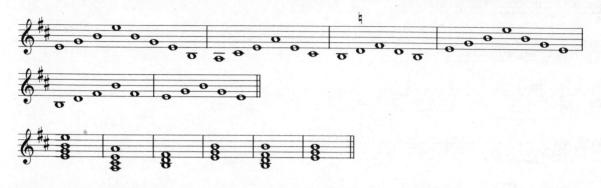

Tape 12-14____Harmony

The harmonized melody that you will hear is in the Dorian mode. As you can see from the measures outlined below, the piece has three phrases of eight measures each. The first and last phrases are identical melodically (ABA form) but notice that the harmonization is varied slightly in the third phrase. The key is e Dorian.

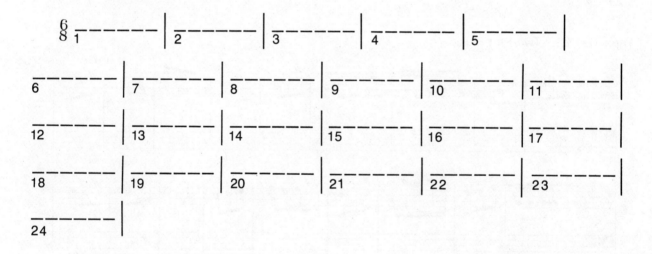

Tape 12-15____Harmony

Three versions of the harmonized melody will be played. Write the bass lines and appropriate chord symbols beneath each note.

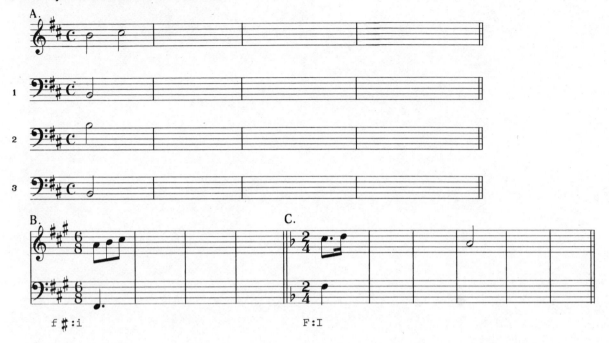

UNIT 13

MODES

Phrygian Mode

Tape 13-1___Listening

A Phrygian scale is performed on Tape 13-1. Add the necessary accidentals in the scale to match the scale played. Write in the key signature and mark the half steps in each tetrachord. Choose other RPs and sing Phrygian scales.

The Phrygian mode creates a distinct aural impression because of the half step between the first and second degrees. It is this factor that makes it easy to identify.

Notice that the second tetrachord has the same pitch arrangement as the *natural minor* with its half step between 5 and 6.

Tape 13-2___Tonal Memory

The number of pitches in the tonal-memory exercises will be increased to eleven beginning with this unit. As before, some of the exercises will be easier than others. If you cannot sing all of the exercises on first hearing, repeat them until you can. The exercises are designed to increase your familiarity with the Phrygian mode and the number of melodic pitches your inner ear can retain.

Exercise 13-1   Intonation: Phrygian Mode

Keep these RPs in your inner ear before singing the exercise.

Exercise 13-2   Mirror Inversion

Sing the melodies as written, then sing in mirror inversion.

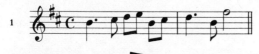

Try performing familiar melodies in inversion. It can be both enjoyable and maddening.

INTERVALS

Tape 13-3____Anticipation: Review of Intervals

The anticipation exercises up to this unit have had an RP followed by one anticipated note. From this point on the anticipation exercises will involve two notes to be sung after the RP. These expanded drills should improve sight singing.

Tape 13-4____Error Correction: Intervals

On the first hearing jot down the symbol for the correct interval in the measures where there are errors, then revise the notation when the tape is finished. The lower note is always correct.

Tape 13-5____Error Correction: Melody

Study this melody before playing the tape. Mark all rhythmic and melodic errors heard when the tape is played. Later, write the notes played incorrectly on the staff.

Lower note is always correct

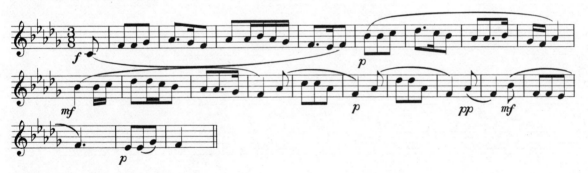

CONFERENCE: Multiple RPs.

Earlier it was mentioned that you should strive to recall as many *reference pitches* as possible. In the first intonation exercises and in Rehearsed Melodies one and sometimes two RPs have been given. There are techniques that you will find valuable in increasing the number of RPs you can retain.

1. Write out on the chart printed below the major, three minor, and modal scales. Practice singing the scales two ways:

a. as scales, up and down; and

b. skipping from one note to any other note until the inner ear considers every scale degree an RP.

2. Include in the chart following each scale the principal chords of that scale—those studied thus far (and add others later). Sing the chords in all their configurations and fuse them in progressions similar to Exercise 11-7 or, better yet, exercises you have composed.

Major (Ionian)

Natural Minor (Aeolian)

Melodic Minor

Harmonic Minor

Mixolydian

Dorian

Phrygian

Lydian

HARMONY

Secondary Triads

The remaining diatonic triads, vi, ii, and iii are called secondary triads, the I, IV, and V being primary. (The vii° partakes so much of the quality and function of V7 that it is often viewed as a variation of dominant harmony.) Indeed, the primary triads are stronger in effect than the secondary; further, the primary triads are found with greater frequency.

In addition to their characteristic functions, the secondary triads can be identified by their quality. In major keys, where the I, IV, and V are all major, the ii, vi, and iii are minor. In minor, i and iv are minor, VI is major, ii is diminished, and iii is major or augmented.*

Secondary triads function in two ways. First, they may appear as chords in their own right. In this case, their pattern of occurence often follows the *circle of fifths* (No. 1).

*Augmented triads will be discussed in advanced ear training.

I   IV   vii° iii   vi   ii   V   I

Another function of secondary triads is as a substitute for a primary triad. Thus, occasionally a vi triad will stand in place of I at the end of a phrase preceded by V or V7. This is called the *deceptive cadence*.

Here it is clear that vi is replacing the tonic—assuming the function of the tonic. This standard "deception" is usually resolved in the next phrase with the V7 resolving to the anticipated I.

vi

The deceptive cadence also occurs in minor, where the VI is major.

CONFERENCE: Listening Goals

Our goal for the remainder of Volume I is to learn to identify all of the diatonic triads and the dominant seventh. In most of the exercises the chords will appear in "normal" sequence, i.e., following rather traditional progression patterns. However, in some cases the progressions are atypical. Therefore, be alert: do not assume that progressions will always follow the pattern you may anticipate. Also, depending on the textbook or approach your theory class uses, you may not be equally familiar with all of the chords used here. Even so, if you can identify major and minor triads and their inversions you should be able to recognize aurally all of the harmonic materials employed in this book.

Tape 13-6____Listening with Notation: VI Chord

Listen to the following progressions, with notation and, later, without looking at the notation.

1. I vi IV V7 I   3. I IV V7 vi I⁶₄ V7 I
2. i VI iv V7 i   4. i iv V7 VI i⁶₄ V7 i

Exercise 13-3   Fusing: Function

Sing the melodic version of these harmonic progressions until the transition to vertical hearing is accomplished.

Tape 13-7____Aural Recognition: Review of Chords

Abstract chords in root position and inversions will be played. Write the symbols that indicate quality and inversion.

1	2	3	4	5
6	7	8	9	10
11	12	13	14	15
16	17	18	19	20

Exercise 13-4   Visual Recognition: Chords

With the metronome set at 120, identify the chord and inversion, allowing four clicks for each.

Tape 13-8____Anticipation: Harmony

After the RP has sounded in each measure, hear the chord that follows. The tape will play the chord afterward.

A.

B.

Tape 13-9___Fusing: Harmony

The melody with bass shown here makes use of the I$^6_4$, V7, and vi chords. Learn the two parts separately, then fuse. As you can see, the lower part is a bass line in its simplest form. Write in the symbols where you hear implied chord changes in your inner ear. When you can hear both parts and the implied harmonies in your mind, then play the tape and compare. It is possible that the chords you anticipated may not coincide with those played, since more than one harmonization is possible from the two given parts. If this happens analyze the chord progressions that differed before turning to the answer section.

Tape 13-10___Error Correction: Harmony

Study, fuse, and hear vertically these short exercises before they are played on the tape. Mark and correct errors in quality, inversion, or function. Each example is played four times, each time with different errors.

a.

1 __ __ __   __ __ __ __   __ __ __
2 __ __ __   __ __ __   __ __ __
3 __ __ __   __ __ __   __ __ __
4 __ __ __   __ __ __   __ __ __

b.

1 __ __ __   __ __ __ __
2 __ __ __   __ __ __ __
3 __ __ __   __ __ __ __
4 __ __ __   __ __ __ __

The music below is an ensemble from Unit 8. On this tape it will be performed with rhythmic and melodic errors. If this ensemble is one not studied in Unit 8, learn it before playing the tape. (It might be a good idea to review it in the inner ear even if it was learned earlier.)

Circle and identify the mistakes.

RHYTHM

Mixed Basic Durations

In some music one encounters meter changes that involve basic durations of varying length. These mixed BDs add rhythmic interest but are tricky and require thought and preparation. In these instances there is usually a lower rhythmic level at which the two BDs have a unit in common.

In this case, the notation (♪ = ♪) makes clear that the *eighth note* is the common unit. Without this notation it would not be certain whether the BD

(♩ = ♩.) or the division (♪ = ♪) remained constant. If the BD remained constant (♩ = ♩.) it would be an example of the mixed levels discussed in

Unit 12. Musicians must be able to perform both—mixed levels or mixed basic durations.

The aural impression when moving from $\frac{2}{4}$ to $\frac{6}{8}$ using mixed BDs is of slowing down, even though the eighth notes are exactly the same duration. Intone the next example and notice what happens when the meters are reversed so that $\frac{6}{8}$ precedes $\frac{2}{4}$.

216

CONFERENCE: Comparison of Mixed Levels and Mixed BDs

The two key words to remember from Unit 12 and Unit 13 discussions of rhythm are *level* and *duration*.

In mixed levels the *pulse* is *constant* even though the divisions change.

In mixed basic durations the *pulse shifts,* faster or slower, although there may be a common rhythmic unit between the two BDs.

Composers in the twentieth century have been more careful in marking rhythmic changes than composers in previous eras. In earlier music, it is sometimes not clear what is intended; consequently, the performer must use his or her best judgment. Sometimes it may be necessary to consult a textbook that deals with the performance practice of the particular period.

Exercise 13-5   Rhythm: Mixed BDs

Perform each of the following exercises at various tempos. Also, perform them both ways, as mixed BDs or mixed levels, and decide which you prefer.

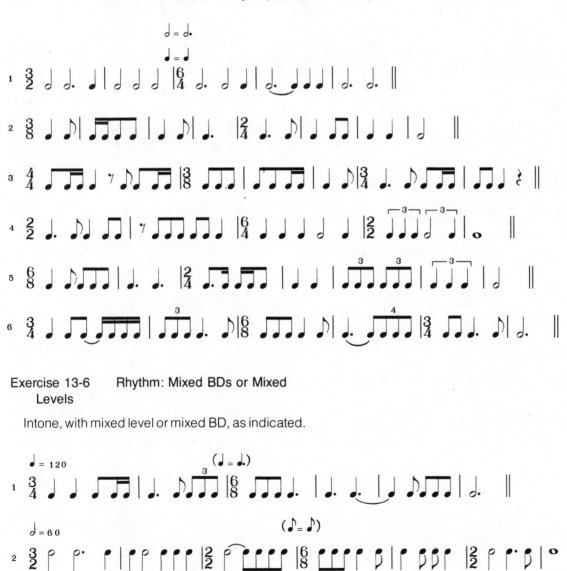

Exercise 13-6   Rhythm: Mixed BDs or Mixed Levels

Intone, with mixed level or mixed BD, as indicated.

Tape 13-12_____Error Correction: Rhythm

Write corrections where errors occur.

Exercise 13-7   Scanning

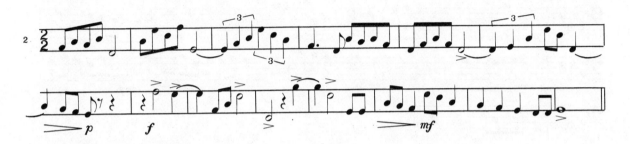

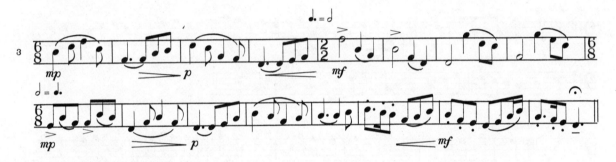

REHEARSED MELODIES

Allegro

Dvořák

ENSEMBLES

SIGHT-READING

MORE DIFFICULT

DICTATION

Melody

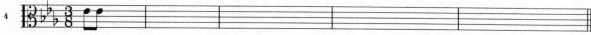

For additional practice in dictation replay Tape 13-2.

Bach

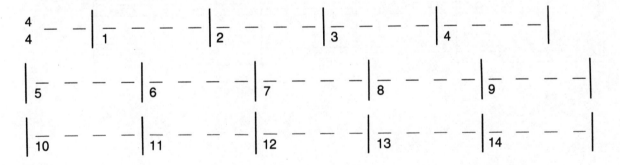

Tape 13-15____Harmony

The I, IV, V7 and I$^6_4$, and vi chords are found in this harmonization of a melody in E-flat major. Notice the momentary quality change in measure nine to accommodate the flatted melodic interval.

$\frac{4}{4}$ — — | 1 — — — — | 2 — — — | 3 — — — — | 4 — — — — |

| 5 — — — — | 6 — — — — | 7 — — — — | 8 — — — — | 9 — — — — |

| 10 — — — — | 11 — — — — | 12 — — — — | 13 — — — — | 14 — — — — |

Write the melody, bass lines, and chord symbols
beneath each of the three versions of this harmonized
melody. The bass line played by the cello will help
identify the inversions.

A.

B.

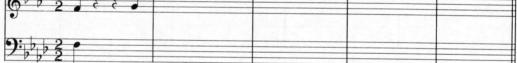

UNIT 14

HARMONY

ii Chord

In major keys the ii adds another minor chord to the harmonic spectrum. A ii–V–I progression is as common in music as IV–V–I. Note the motion of the bass in ii–V–I.

B♭ : ii V7 I

The ii stands in the relationship of the dominant to the V chord, which has the dominant relationship to the tonic. When the ii chord is found in first inversion the similarity to the IV–V–I progression is emphasized.

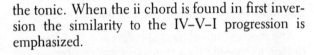

Tape 14-1____Listening with Notation: ii Chord

During the first playing of this tape listen and follow along with the chord symbols printed below. With the next playing, look away and hear the function of the harmonies.

1. I IV V I
2. I ii V I
3. I ii6 V I
4. I vi ii V7 I
5. I IV ii6 V7 I

Exercise 14-1   Fusing: Harmony—ii Chord

Once again here are melodic versions of harmonies that should eventually be heard as chords in the inner ear. Remember, the faster you can sing No. 1 the closer you come to the goal of hearing the chordal version in No. 2.

Tape 14-2 _____ Aural Recognition: Review of Chords

Write the symbols for the root position and inverted abstract chords played on this tape.

1	2	3	4	5
6	7	8	9	10
11	12	13	14	15
16	17	18	19	20

Exercise 14-2   Visual Recognition: Chords

The metronome setting should be 112. Allow four pulses to identify the chord and the inversion.

Tape 14-3 _____ Anticipation: Harmony

After the RP is played, hear the chord shown. The tape will play the chord before the next RP so you can check what your inner ear heard.

Tape 14-4____Fusing: Harmony

Interesting uses of secondary chords ii and vi will be heard in this harmonization.

Follow the same procedure for hearing this piece as you have in previous units: learn the top part and bass line separately, then fuse. In the process, harmonies will begin to suggest themselves. Fill in chord symbols until the harmony is completed. When you can hear the two parts and harmonies, compare the tape's version with yours. Write in the tape's chords where they vary from yours.

If you have difficulty hearing the chords in the progression you work out from the bass and soprano, write out your harmonic progression in the form used in Exercise 14-1.

Tape 14-5____Error Correction: Harmony

First learn the original four-measure example. The tape will play four different versions. Circle and correct chords where changes appear.

Original

Tape 14-6_____Error Correction: Two-Part Music

The ensemble shown here was one presented in Unit 8. Review it in the inner ear before playing the tape, even if it was one learned previously. If you did not learn it earlier, study the ensemble following the procedures recommended in the conference dealing with ensembles, p.36.

Praetorius

MODES

Lydian Mode

Tape 14-7_____Listening: Lydian Mode

1. Write in the necessary accidentals.
2. Mark half and whole steps.
3. Write key signature.

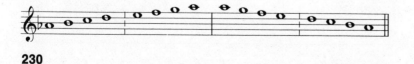

The Lydian scale is readily identified because of the whole-tone structure of the first tetrachord. Notice that the first half step occurs *between* the first and second tetrachord (4 and 5).

Lydian's second tetrachord is the same as the second tetrachord in *major* with the half step between 7 and 8.

Tape 14-8____Tonal Memory

The number of pitches heard in this tonal-memory exercise will be increased to twelve; otherwise it is the same type of exercise you have sung previously.

Exercise 14-3   Intonation: Lydian Mode

Retain these RPs in your inner ear before starting this exercise.

CONFERENCE: Similarities and Differences in Modes

Students sometimes have difficulty differentiating the modes; let us summarize the problem.

All modes may be grouped in *two* categories, major or minor, when the first tetrachords are considered:

1. Major—Lydian, Mixolydian, Ionian
2. Minor—Dorian, Phrygian, Aeolian

Modes with similar second tetrachords fall into *three* groups.

1. Lydian, Ionian—half steps between 7 and 8
2. Phrygian, Aeolian—half steps between 5 and 6
3. Dorian, Mixolydian—half steps between 6 and 7

In addition, remember the other distinguishing characteristics of the separate modes:

Dorian—the raised sixth degree that colors its minor quality;

Phrygian—the half step between 1 and 2 which is its aural trademark;

Lydian—with its major-scale quality except for the raised fourth degree;

231

Mixolydian—the same as major except for the lowered seventh degree;

Ionian—the same as major;

Aeolian—the same as natural minor.

There are other modes and scales in use in music but they are less common. Two are shown below, which you should sing.

The Locrian mode has half steps between 1 and 2 and between 4 and 5.

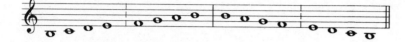

The Gypsy scale has half steps between 2 and 3, 4 and 5, 5 and 6, and 7 and 8. Notice the augmented seconds that appear between 3 and 4 and 6 and 7 that create this scale's exotic sound.

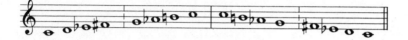

Three more scales deserve mention: chromatic, pentatonic, and whole tone. The pentatonic scale will be taken up in Unit 15; however, the whole-tone scale will be deferred until the second book.

INTERVALS

Tape 14-9____Anticipation: Review of Intervals

In each measure sing the three notes following the RP. If you cannot sing them perfectly at the first playing, repeat this exercise.

Tape 14-10____Error Correction: Intervals

Some of the intervals printed below will be incorrect when you hear the tape. When this happens the upper note that is heard will be correct. If you are fast at recognizing intervals write in the notes as you go along; otherwise jot down the symbol for the interval, then return later and write the notes which should appear on the staff.

Tape 14-11___Error Correction: Rhythm

The rhythms played on the tape and those on the page will not always match. Circle the measures where errors appear, then write in the corrections.

Tape 14-12___Error Correction: Melody

Learn this Lydian melody before playing the tape. Circle and correct errors in rhythm and melody where they appear.

REHEARSED RHYTHM

Intone the following exercises at the speeds indicated.

REHEARSED MELODIES

Mendoza

© Copyright G. Schirmer, Inc., New York.
Used by permission of the publisher.

ENSEMBLES

© Copyright Belwin Mills Publishing Corp., Melville, N.Y.
Used by the permission of the publishers

What Mode?

Watch Key Signature

MORE DIFFICULT

♩ = 132

Corigliano, *"Christmas At The Cloisters"*

© Copyright G. Schirmer, Inc., New York.
Used by permission of the publisher.

What Mode?

DICTATION

Tape 14-13____Rhythm

A.

Melody

B.

Difficult!

For additional practice in dictation replay Tape 14-8.

C.

Tape 14-14____Two-Part Music

Tape 14-15____Harmony

This Aeolian melody presents interesting possibilities for the use of the ii chord, which is diminished. Also listen for the dominant, which is sometimes minor and at other times major. The VI—major in this case—and the iv chord are also present. If you listen for chord quality and the bass line, this will not be a difficult dictation exercise.

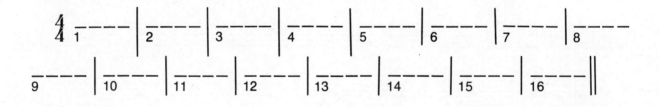

Tape 14-16_____Harmony

Three different harmonizations of this melody will be played. Write melody, the bass lines, and chord symbols for each.

UNIT 15

PENTATONIC SCALES

Although the pentatonic scales are often associated with music of Oriental cultures, a surprising amount of Western music (American Indian, Celtic, Scottish) employs five-tone musical systems with scales comprised of whole tones and minor thirds, without minor seconds.

There are five of these more common pentatonic scales.* Each begins on a black key of the piano keyboard and uses *only* black keys. (All other modes may be compared to those beginning on a particular white key of the keyboard and using only white keys.)

Pentatonic Scales	Interval Patterns				
	1	2	3	4	5
	M2	m3	M2	M2	m3
	m3	M2	M2	m3	M2
	M2	M2	m3	M2	m3
	M2	m3	M2	m3	M2
	m3	M2	m3	M2	M2

*Other pentatonic scales exist, which do contain halfsteps. We are dealing here only with the category known as tonal (anhemitonic) pentatonic scales.

Exercise 15-1　　Singing Pentatonic Scales

Sing each of the pentatonic scales shown above, starting on the various pitches.

Exercise 15-2　　Visual Recognition: Scales

Sing and identify the following scales from the interval pattern.

1. m2 M2 M2 M2 m2 M2 M2 _____
2. M2 M2 m2 M2 M2 m2 M2 _____
3. M2 m2 M2 M2 M2 m2 M2 _____
4. M2 M2 M2 m2 M2 M2 m2 _____
5. M2 M2 m2 M2 M2 M2 m2 _____
6. M2 m2 M2 M2 m2 M2 M2 _____

Tape 15-1____Tonal Memory

Five melodies will be played on this tape, many using pentatonic scales. If you cannot sing back all of the melodies without error, replay the tape until you can.

Exercise 15-3　　Intonation: Pentatonic Scale

INTERVALS

Tape 15-2____Anticipation: Review of Intervals

After the RP is sounded, sing the pitches that are written in each measure. The tape will play them after you have sung.

Tape 15-3____Error Correction: Intervals

The intervals shown may not be correct. When there is a difference between what is seen and what is heard, circle the interval and write the correct symbol. The highest given note will always be correct.

Tape 15-4____Error Correction: Melody

Learn this folksong before it is played on the tape. Note the errors and write them on the staff.

Exercise 15-4   Intonation: Modes

1. Sing the following at a comfortable tempo. Identify the scale type, ascending and descending.

2. The altered degrees in the intonation exercise can all be related to the RPs given immediately below.

Tape 15-5———Aural Recognition: Modes

A four-measure melody will be played six times, each time in a different mode. Indicate the mode by writing D, P, L, M, A, or I after the numbers.

Before playing the tape, review the characteristics of all the modes.

    1   2   3   4   5   6

HARMONY

iii Chord

The iii (III) chord is the last diatonic chord to be discussed in this book.

In a *major* key the *quality* of the iii chord is minor; whereas the quality in *natural minor* is major.

Tape 15-6____Listening with Notation: iii Chord

In previous units it was recommended that you listen first, watching the symbols of the chords. This time listen without referring to the page and see if you can identify the iii chord as well as the other chords in the progression.

1. I iii vi IV I$^6_4$ V7 I

2. i III VI iv i$^6_4$ V7 i

3. I IV V7 iii vi IV6 V7 I

4. I iii IV V7 I

Exercise 15-5   Fusing: Function—iii Chord

Practice No. 1 at faster and faster speeds until the transition from the melodic version to the harmonic progression (No. 2) is accomplished.

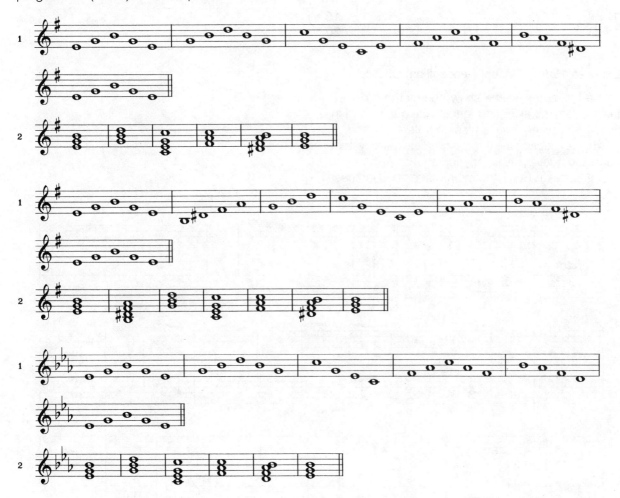

Tape 15-7____Aural Recognition: Review of Chords

All of the chords studied thus far will be included in this review tape. Write the symbols for the quality and inversion (if there is one) after the numerals below.

1	2	3	4	5
6	7	8	9	10
11	12	13	14	15
16	17	18	19	20

Exercise 15-6   Visual Recognition: Chords

The first two systems show abstract chords. Set the metronome at 76 and identify the quality and inversion, allowing three pulses per item.

When executing the examples in the third system, name the quality, inversion, and chord symbol in the key of G major. Reset the metronome at 60 for these chords.

Tape 15-8_____Anticipation: Harmony

Try to anticipate each chord from the RP.

Tape 15-9_____Fusing: Harmony

The folksong shown here uses the secondary chords discussed earlier—ii, iii, and vi. Hear the melody and bass lines separately before attempting to fuse. In the process of fusing the two parts harmonies will undoubtedly be implied in your inner ear. Note these implied chord progressions under the bass part before playing the version on the tape. As was mentioned in earlier units, the tape version and your version may not match because there is latitude for differences. However, try your version on the piano or guitar before listening to the tape, then compare.

Errors in harmony will occur in each of the six examples. Your procedure should be to analyze and hear inwardly each of the brief progressions. Then play the tape and note on the staff the specific differences.

Tape 15-11____Error Correction: Two-Part Music

Mark where errors occur. Identify exact rhythmic or
melodic errors.

RHYTHM

Tape 15-12____Error Correction: Rhythm

Write the correct rhythms above the measure
where the tape differs from what is printed.

Exercise 15-7   Scanning

REHEARSED RHYTHM

Intone the following rhythmic exercises at the
tempos given.

REHEARSED MELODIES

Korean Folksong

American Lullaby

ENSEMBLES

SIGHT-READING

Okinawan Folksong

MORE DIFFICULT

Chopin

DICTATION

Tape 15-13____Rhythm

Melody

For additional practice in dictation replay Tape
15-1.

C.

Tape 15-14____Two-Part Music

G. S. Lohlein (Adapted)

Tape 15-15____Harmony

The harmonized melody you will hear is in a mode,
but the scale degree that identifies it is not in the
melody, only the harmony. Can you name the mode?

Observe how the modal scale colors the quality
of the harmonies, particularly the iii chord. Listen also
for interesting uses of inversions.

As before, fill in the chord symbols on the chart.

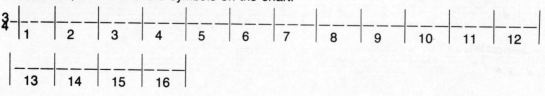

Fill in the soprano and bass parts and the chord symbols for each of the three versions of this harmonized melody.

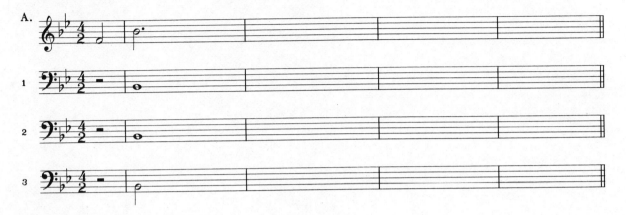

Additional dictation.

ANSWERS

UNIT 1

Exercise 1-5   Note Values: Rhythm

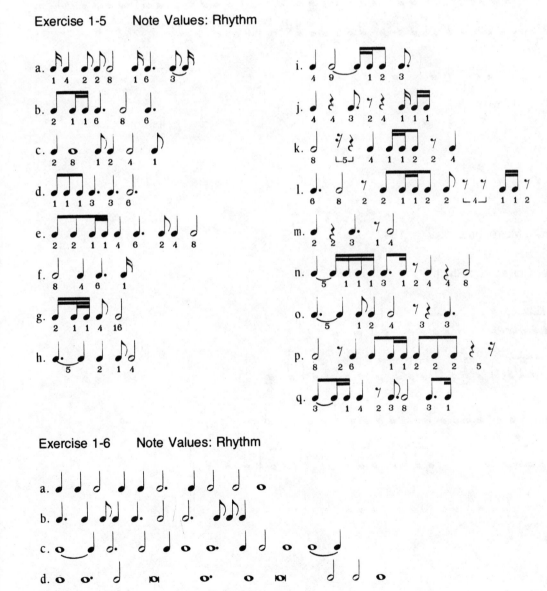

Exercise 1-6   Note Values: Rhythm

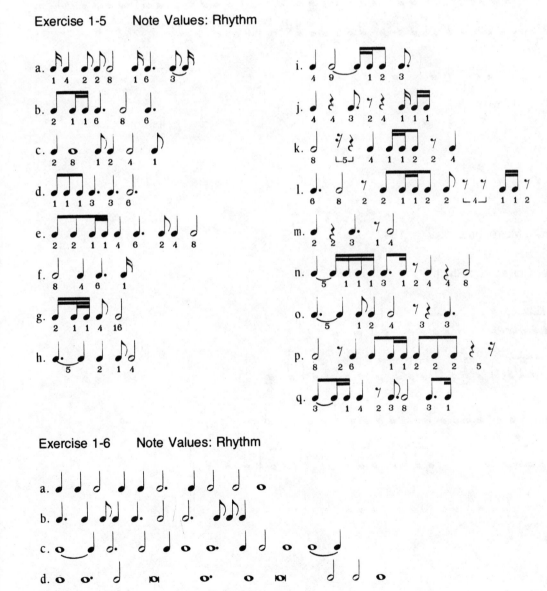

e. [musical notation]

f. [musical notation]

g. [musical notation]

h. [musical notation]

Exercise 1-7   Note Values: Rhythm

a. [musical notation]

b. [musical notation]

c. [musical notation]

d. [musical notation]

e. [musical notation]

UNIT 2

Exercise 2-2   Set Metronome at ♪ = 184.

Tape 2-3   Error Correction: Rhythm

The American folksong "Shenandoah"

Tape 2-4   Dictation: Rhythm

Tape 2-9   Aural Recognition: Seconds

Melodic

1 m2   2   M2   3   M2   4   m2   5   M2
6 m2   7   m2   8   M2   9   m2   10 M2

Harmonic

1 M2   2   m2   3   m2   4   M2   5   M2
6 M2   7   M2   8   m2   9   m2   10 m2

Tape 2-10   Error Correction: Intervals

Tape 2-11   Dictation: Intervals

Tape 2-12   Dictation: Melody, Motives

A.

UNIT 3

Tape 3-6   Aural Recognition

```
1  M3   2   m3   3   m3   4   M3   5   M3
6  M3   7   M3   8   m3   9   M3   10  M3
```

Tape 3-7   Error Correction: Melody

Tape 3-8   Aural Recognition: Review of Intervals

Descending Melodic Intervals

Ascending Melodic Intervals

Harmonic Intervals (Upper Note Given)

Harmonic Intervals (Lower Note Given)

Tape 3-9   Dictation

Rhythm

A.

Melodic Motives

B.

Melody

C.

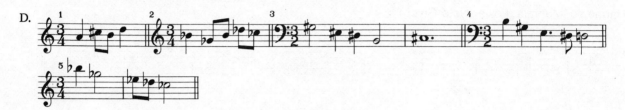

UNIT 4

Exercise 4-1   Note Values

	BD = ♪	BD = ♩
1 + 1 + 1 + 1		
2 + 1 + 1		
1 + 2 + 1		
1 + 1 + 2		
2 + 2		
1 + 3		
3 + 1		

Exercise 4-2   Note Values

268

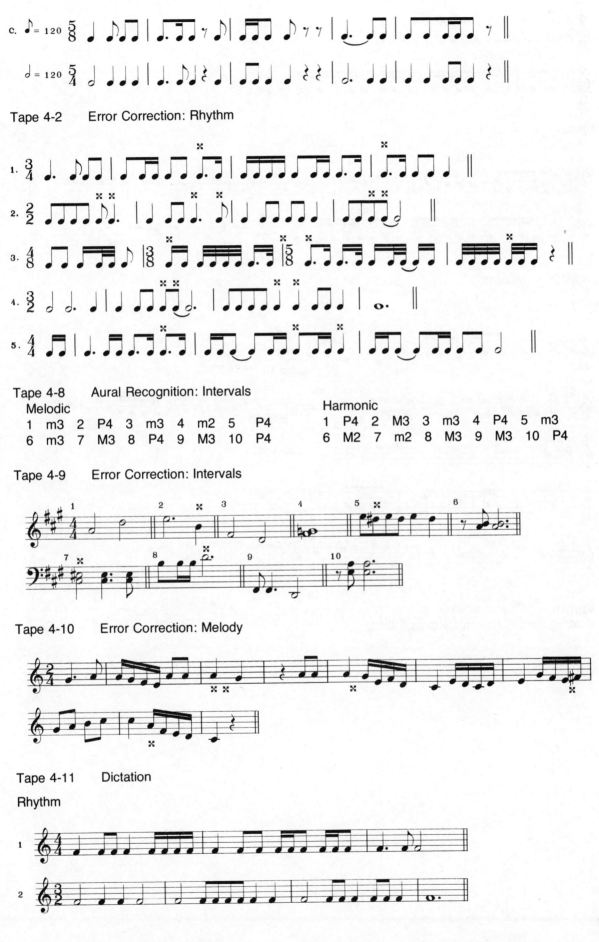

c.

Tape 4-2   Error Correction: Rhythm

1.

2.

3.

4.

5.

Tape 4-8   Aural Recognition: Intervals

Melodic

1	m3	2	P4	3	m3	4	m2	5	P4
6	m3	7	M3	8	P4	9	M3	10	P4

Harmonic

1	P4	2	M3	3	m3	4	P4	5	m3
6	M2	7	m2	8	M3	9	M3	10	P4

Tape 4-9   Error Correction: Intervals

Tape 4-10   Error Correction: Melody

Tape 4-11   Dictation

Rhythm

1.

2.

Motives

Tape 4-12   Dictation

Melody

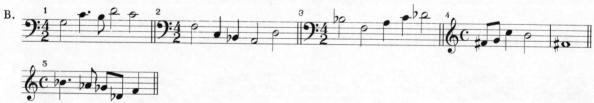

UNIT 5

Exercise 5-1   Meter Signatures

Simple Meters

If the BD is represented by	And there is 1 pulse to the measure the signature is	2 pulses to the measure	3	4	5	6
𝅗𝅥	$\frac{1}{2}$	$\frac{2}{2}$	$\frac{3}{2}$	$\frac{4}{2}$	$\frac{5}{2}$	$\frac{6}{2}$
♩	$\frac{1}{4}$	$\frac{2}{4}$	$\frac{3}{4}$	$\frac{4}{4}$	$\frac{5}{4}$	$\frac{6}{4}$
♪	$\frac{1}{8}$	$\frac{2}{8}$	$\frac{3}{8}$	$\frac{4}{8}$	$\frac{5}{8}$	$\frac{6}{8}$

Compound Meters

If the BD is represented by	And there is 1 pulse to the measure the signature is	2 pulses to the measure	3	4	5	6
𝅗𝅥.	$\frac{3^{*}}{4}$	$\frac{6}{4}$	$\frac{9}{4}$	$\frac{12}{4}$	$\frac{15}{4}$	$\frac{18}{4}$
♩.	$\frac{3}{8}$	$\frac{6}{8}$	$\frac{9}{8}$	$\frac{12}{8}$	$\frac{15}{8}$	$\frac{18}{8}$
♪.	$\frac{3}{16}$	$\frac{6}{16}$	$\frac{9}{16}$	$\frac{12}{16}$	$\frac{15}{16}$	$\frac{18}{16}$

Notice that certain signatures appear in both charts ($\frac{3}{4}$, $\frac{6}{8}$, etc.).

What is the difference between these two signatures?

The number of pulses per measure.
Can the difference be heard in the music?
Yes, usually.

Exercise 5-3   Meter Signatures

	Simple or Compound	Number of BDs per measure
"Parsley, Sage, Rosemary, and Thyme"	C	1
"Home on the Range"	C	1
"Battle Hymn of the Republic"	S	4
"Dixie"	S	2
"Star-Spangled Banner"	S	3
"Irish Washerwoman"	C	2

Exercise 5-4   Note Values

c.

d.

e.

f.

Tape 5-2   Error Correction: Rhythm

a.

b.

c.

Tape 5-8   Aural Recognition: Intervals

Melodic

1	m3	2	P4	3	m3	4	P4	5	m2
6	P5	7	P4	8	M2	9	m3	10	P4

Harmonic

1	M3	2	P5	3	P4	4	M3	5	P5
6	P4	7	M2	8	M3	9	P4	10	m2

Tape 5-9   Error Correction: Melody

Andantino ♩=132

Tape 5-10   Aural Recognition: Triads

1 M	2 M	3 m	4 m	5 M	6 m
7 m	8 m	9 m	10 M	11 m	12 M
13 m	14 m	15 m			

Tape 5-11   Error Correction: Triads

Only incorrect triads shown.

Tape 5-14   Error Correction: Two-Part Music

Tape 5-15   Dictation: Rhythm

Tape 5-16   Dictation

Motives

A.

Melody

B.

C.

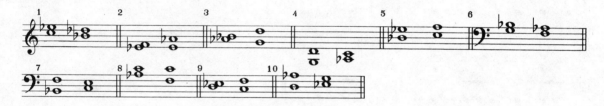

Tape 5-17   Dictation: Two-Part Music

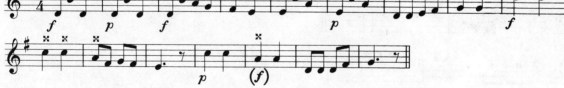

UNIT 6

Tape 6-6   Aural Recognition: Review of Intervals

Melodic
1 P5 2 P4 3 M6 4 M2 5 m3
6 M6 7 M3 8 P5 9 M2 10 m6

Harmonic
1 M6 2 M2 3 P5 4 M6 5 P4
6 M6 7 M3 8 P5 9 M6 10 P5

Tape 6-7   Error Correction: Melody

Tape 6-12   Aural Recognition: Harmony

New melodies.

Exercise 6-6   Harmonizing Folksongs

"Down In The Valley"

"Bridge At Avignon"

Tape 6-13   Dictation: Rhythm

Tape 6-14   Dictation

Motives

Melody

Tape 6-15   Dictation: Two-Part Music

Tape 6-16   Dictation: Harmony

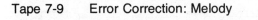

UNIT 7

Tape 7-7   Aural Recognition: Sevenths, Review of Intervals

A.

Melodic and Harmonic—Sevenths

1 M7   2 m7   3 M7   4 m7   5 m7
6 M7   7 m7   8 M7   9 M7   10 m7

B.

Melodic—Review of Intervals

1 P4   2 M3   3 M7   4 P5   5 m6
6 P5   7 M7   8 M6   9 m2   10 M7

Harmonic

1 M2   2 m7   3 P5   4 P4   5 M7
6 m2   7 M6   8 M3   9 m7   10 m6

Tape 7-8   Error Correction: Intervals

Only corrected intervals listed.

2 P4   5 m3   7 m3   8 M3   10 m2
14 P4   15 m6   17 m6   19 M3   20 m2

Tape 7-9   Error Correction: Melody

Tape 7-13   Error Correction: Two-Part Music

Tape 7-14   Dictation

Rhythm

A.

Melody

B.

Tape 7-15   Dictation: Two-Part Music

Tape 7-16   Dictation: Harmony

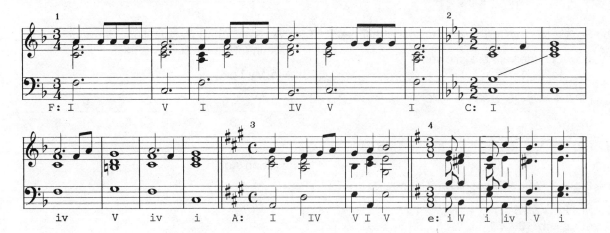

UNIT 8

Tape 8-6   Aural Recognition: Interval Review

Melodic	Harmonic
1 T 2 M3 3 M6 4 m2 5 m7	1 m3 2 P5 3 M3 4 M2 5 m7
6 P4 7 M3 8 T 9 M2 10 T	6 P4 7 T 8 m3 9 m6 10 m2

Tape 8-7   Error Correction: Review of Intervals

Melodic (Only corrected intervals shown.)	Harmonic (Only corrected intervals shown.)
2 m6 5 T 6 P4 8 m2 12 P4	3 m7 4 M2 7 m7

Tape 8-12   Aural Recognition: Intervals

a. Ascending melodic intervals. Lower note given.

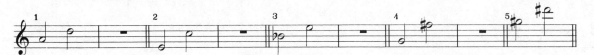

b. Harmonic intervals. Lower note given.

c. Descending melodic intervals. Upper note given.

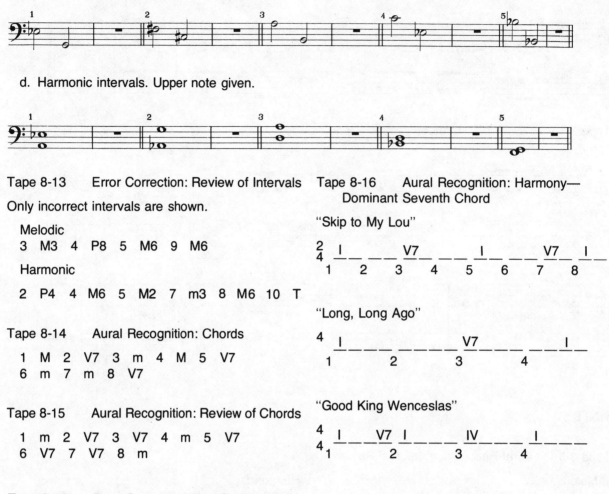

d. Harmonic intervals. Upper note given.

Tape 8-13   Error Correction: Review of Intervals

Only incorrect intervals are shown.

Melodic
3 M3 4 P8 5 M6 9 M6

Harmonic

2 P4 4 M6 5 M2 7 m3 8 M6 10 T

Tape 8-14   Aural Recognition: Chords

1 M 2 V7 3 m 4 M 5 V7
6 m 7 m 8 V7

Tape 8-15   Aural Recognition: Review of Chords

1 m 2 V7 3 V7 4 m 5 V7
6 V7 7 V7 8 m

Tape 8-16   Aural Recognition: Harmony— Dominant Seventh Chord

"Skip to My Lou"

$\frac{2}{4}$ I ___ ___ V7 ___ ___ I ___ ___ V7 ___ I ___
  1   2   3   4   5   6   7   8

"Long, Long Ago"

$\frac{4}{4}$ I ___ ___ ___ ___ ___ ___ V7 ___ ___ ___ ___ I ___
  1   2   3   4

"Good King Wenceslas"

$\frac{4}{4}$ I ___ ___ V7 I ___ ___ ___ IV ___ ___ ___ I ___ ___ ___
  1   2   3   4

Tape 8-17   Error Correction: Two-Part Music

280

Rhythm

A.

Melody

B.

C.

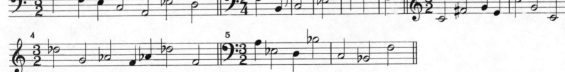

Andante   J. S. Bach

Tape 8-20   Dictation: Harmony

UNIT 9

Exercise 9-1

283

Tape 9-2   Error Correction: Rhythm

Tape 9-6   Aural Recognition: Review of Intervals

Melodic									
1	P5	2	M6	3	M6	4	M7	5	m7
6	m2	7	M2	8	M3	9	P4	10	M7

Harmonic									
1	T	2	M6	3	M2	4	m2	5	m2
6	M6	7	m6	8	T	9	M7	10	P4

Tape 9-7   Error Correction: Melody

Tape 9-9   Aural Recognition: Root Position and First Inversion Triads

1 M_3^6 2 m_3^5 3 m_3^5 4 m_3^6 5 M_3^5

6 m_3^6 7 m_3^5 8 M_3^5 9 m_3^5 10 m_3^6

11 m_3^6 12 M_3^5

Tape 9-12   Error Correction: Harmony

Tape 9-13   Two-Part Music

1 C C   2 P C   3 S C   4 O C   5 O C
6 C S   7 P O   8 O C   9 S C   10 C C

Tape 9-14   Error Correction: Two-Part Music

Tape 9-15   Dictation

Rhythm

Melody

285

Tape 9-16   Dictation: Two-Part Music

Tape 9-17   Dictation: Harmony

A.

286

UNIT 10

Tape 10-5   Aural Recognition: Review of Intervals

Melodic   Harmonic

1 m3 2 m6 3 P4 4 m7 5 m2   1 m2 2 P5 3 P8 4 T 5 M6

6 P5 7 M3 8 M7 9 M6 10 T   6 M3 7 m6 8 M2 9 P4 10 M7

Tape 10-6   Error Correction: Melody

Tape 10-8   Aural Recognition: Harmony   Tape 10-10   Harmony: Function

1 V 2 V7 3 V7 4 V 5 V_5^6 1 vii°6 2 V_5^6 3 V_5^6 4 vii°

6 V6 7 V_3^5 8 V_5^6 5 V 6 V_5^6 7 vii° 8 V7

Tape 10-12   Error Correction: Harmony

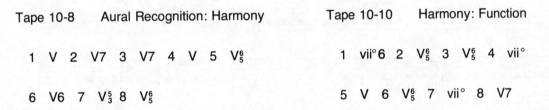

Tape 10-13   Error Correction: Two-Part Music

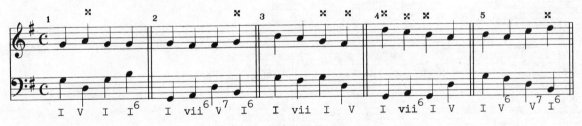

Praetorius

Tape 10-14   Dictation

Rhythm

Melody

C.

Tape 10-15   Dictation: Two-Part Music

Tape 10-16   Dictation: Harmony

$\frac{3}{4}$ V i | i6 V | V $^6_5$ i | iv i | i6 iv | iv 6 | V7 i
— — | — — | — — | — — | — — | — — | — —
1   2   3   4   5   6   7

$\frac{6}{4}$ V7 V | $^6_5$ i | i6 V7 | V $^6_5$ | i | V $^6_5$ i | V | V $^6_5$ i i | $^6_4$ V7 I
8   9   10   11   12   13   14   15   16

Tape 10-17   Dictation: Harmony

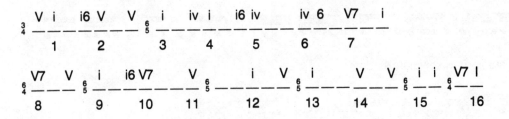

A.

1   I   V6   I   IV6   I   V   I   VI   V   I

2   I   V   I   IV   I   V6   I   vii6   I6   V   I

3   I   V   I   V7   I   V5   I   V   I6   V   I

UNIT 11

Tape 11-1   Error Correction: Rhythm

Tape 11-2   Listening: Mixolydian Mode

Tape 11-5   Error Correction: Review of Intervals

Tape 11-6   Error Correction: Melody

Schuetz

Tape 11-10   Aural Recognition: Chords

A. 1. V^7; 2. m_4^6; 3. m_3^5; 4. m_3^5; 5. M_3^5;
   6. m_4^6; 7. V^7; 8. m_4^6; 9. V^7; 10. M_3^5;
   11. vii^{o6}; 12. M_3^5; 13. V_5^6; 14. V_3^4;
   15. V_3^4; 16. V_3^4; 17. m_3^6; 18. V_5^6;
   19. m_4^6; 20. V_5^6;

B. 1. 3; 2. 8; 3. 8; 4. 3; 5. 5;
   6. 5; 7. 8; 8. 5; 9. 3; 10. 3;
   11. 8; 12. 5; 13. 7; 14. 7; 15. 3;
   16. 8; 17. 8; 18. 7; 19. 8; 20. 8.

Tape 11-12   Error Correction: Harmony

Tape 11-13   Dictation

Rhythm

Melody

Tape 11-14   Dictation: Two-Part Music

UNIT 12

Tape 12-2   Aural Recognition: Review of Chords

1 M_3^6 2 V_2^4 3 M 4 M_3^6 5 V_5^6 6 m_4^6 7 m 8 $_3^4$ 9 m 10 M_4^6

11 V_2^4 12 V_3^4 13 m 14 m_4^6 15 m 16 m_4^6 17 M_3^6 18 M 19 V_3^4 20 V_2^4

Tape 12-4   Error Correction: Harmony

Tape 12-5   Listening: Dorian Scale

The scale shown *is* Dorian; therefore, no sharps or
flats are needed.

Tape 12-8   Error Correction: Intervals

Tape 12-9   Error Correction: Melody

Tape 12-10   Error Correction: Two-Part Music

Tape 12-12   Dictation

Rhythm

A.

Melody

B.

Frescobaldi

C.

Tape 12-13   Dictation: Two-Part Music

A. Scarlatti

Tape 12-14   Dictation: Harmony

i	i	i v	i v	i
1	2	3	4	5
i v	i v	i	i	IV i
6	7	8	9	10
v	i v i	i	IV i IV v	i v
11	12	13	14	15
i	i IV v	i	IV i	IV v i v
16	17	18	19	20
i IV v	i v	i v	I	
21	22	23	24	

Tape 12-15   Dictation: Harmony

A.

B.

f :   i   i⁶   iv   V   V²   i⁶   V⁴₃   i

C.

F♯:   I   V   I⁶   V   vii⁶   V⁷   I   IV   V   I

UNIT 13

Tape 13-1   Listening: Phrygian Mode

Tape 13-4   Error Correction: Intervals

Tape 13-5 Error Correction: Melody

Tape 13-7 Harmony: Review of Chords

1 d_4^6 2 M_3^6 3 M_4^6 4 m 5 M_3^6 6 V_3^4 7 d_4^6 8 M 9 V7 10 d_3^6

11 M_3^6 12 m_3^6 13 M_4^6 14 M_4^6 15 M_3^6 16 V_3^4 17 M 18 d_3^6 19 m_3^6 20 V7

Tape 13-9 Fusing: Harmony

I I^6 IV   I IV   I   I V   I IV I_4^6 V^7 I

I   I   V V   I IV V V   vi   vi IV I_4^6 V^7 I

Tape 13-10 Error Correction: Harmony

A.

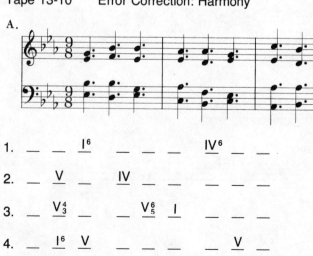

1. __ __ I^6 __ __ IV^6 __ __

2. __ V __ IV __ __ __ __

3. __ V_3^4 __ __ V_5^6 I __ __ __

4. __ I^6 V __ __ __ V __

298

B.

1. __ V⁶ i __ __ __ __ S: E / A: G

2. __ __ V₂⁴ i⁶ __ __ I S: G#

3. __ __ V₂⁴ i⁶ __ __ T: F#

4. __ iv i __ __ __ __ S: E / T: E

Tape 13-11   Error Correction: Two-Part Music

Tape 13-12   Error Correction: Rhythm

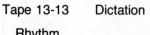

Tape 13-13   Dictation

Rhythm

Melody

Tape 13-14   Dictation: Two-Part Music

Tape 13-15   Dictation: Harmony

Tape 13-16   Dictation: Harmony

A.

B.

C.

Tape 14-2   Aural Recognition: Review of Chords

1 M$_4^6$ 2 m 3 V7 4 M$_3^6$ 5 V$_2^4$ 6 V$_5^6$ 7 m$_4^6$ 8 M 9 V$_2^4$ 10 d$_3^6$

11 M$_4^6$ 12 m 13 m 14 m$_4^6$ 15 V7 16 V$_2^4$ 17 M 18 m 19 m 20 M

Tape 14-4   Fusing: Harmony

Tape 14-5   Error Correction: Harmony

302

Tape 14-6   Error Correction: Two-Part Music

Praetorius

Tape 14-7   Listening: Lydian Mode

Tape 14-10   Error Correction: Intervals

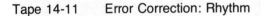

Tape 14-11   Error Correction: Rhythm

Tape 14-12   Error Correction: Melody

Tape 14-13   Dictation: Rhythm

A.

Melody

B.

Tape 14-14   Dictation: Two-Part Music

Tape 14-15   Dictation: Harmony

Tape 14-16   Dictation: Harmony

C.

$B\flat$:I V^6 V^7 vi V^4_2 V^6_5 I vii^6 V^7 I

UNIT 15

Exercise 15-2   Identification of Scales

1. Phrygian
2. Mixolydian
3. Dorian
4. Lydian
5. Major
6. Natural Minor

Tape 15-3   Error Correction: Intervals

Tape 15-4   Error Correction: Melody

English Folksong

Exercise 15-4   Intonation: Modes

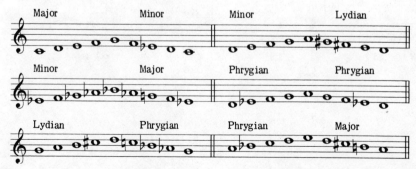

306

Tape 15-5 Aural Recognition: Modes

1 L 2 I 3 A 4 D 5 P 6 M

Tape 15-7 Aural Recognition: Review of Chords

1 V_5^6 2 m 3 M 4 m_4^6 5 m 6 V_5^6 7 V_2^4 8 m 9 M_4^6 10 m

11 m 12 M_3^6 13 M_4^6 14 M 15 m 16 d 17 V_5^6 18 m 19 M_4^6 20 V_2^4

Tape 15-9 Fusing: Harmony

Tape 15-10 Error Correction: Harmony

307

Tape 15-11   Error Correction: Two-Part Music

Tape 15-12   Rhythm: Error Correction

Tape 15-13   Dictation: Rhythm

A.

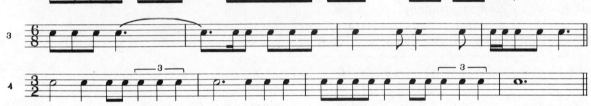

Melody

B.

C.

Tape 15-15   Dictation: Harmony

IV i   v III IV i   v v6 i v i6 v v6 i v

$\frac{3}{4}$

1   2   3   4   5   6   7

i   v i i6 v i   i6 IV i v   III i6 v i   i6 IV V   I

8   9   10   11   12   13   14   15   16

PROGRESS CHART

Page	UNIT 1	Com-pleted	An-swers	Comments
	PITCH			
	Matching Pitches, Reference Pitch			
	Conference: On Conferences			
	Tape 1-1 Matching Pitches			
	Conference: Octave Displacement			
	Tonal Memory			
	Tape 1-2 Tonal Memory			
	RHYTHM			
	Pulse, Basic Duration, and Count			
	Ex. 1-1 Basic Duration			
	Tones and Rests of One BD			
	Ex. 1-2 Intoning Rhythm			
	Ex. 1-3 Rehearsed Rhythm			
	Tones and Rests of Two or More BDs			
	Ex. 1-4 Rehearsed Rhythm			
	Note Values			
	Ex. 1-5 Note Values			
	Ex. 1-6 Note Values			
	Ex. 1-7 Rhythmic Notation			
	Conference: Practice with a Partner			
	UNIT 2			
	RHYTHM			
	Counting			
	Tape 2-1 Listening: Rhythm			

Page		Completed	Answers	Comments
	Level 2 Rhythm (Simple Division)			
	Ex. 2-1 Imitation: Rhythm (Level 1 and Level 2)			
	Ex. 2-2 Rehearsed Rhythm			
	Tape 2-2 Anticipation: Rhythm			
	Ex. 2-3 Rehearsed Rhythm: Dotted Rhythms			
	Ex. 2-4 Rehearsed Rhythm			
	Tape 2-3 Error Correction: Rhythm			
	Syncopation and Upbeats			
	Ex. 2-5 Rehearsed Rhythm			
	Ex. 2-6 Rehearsed Rhythm			
	Tape 2-4 Dictation: Rhythm			
	SIGHT-READING			
	Conference: Scanning			
	Ex. 2-7 Scanning			
	Conference: Reference Pitches			
	INTERVALS			
	Seconds—Major and Minor			
	Conference: Singing Seconds			
	Conference: Hearing and Singing Intervals			
	Tape 2-5 Listening: Seconds			
	Conference: Sonority of M2 and m2			
	Ex. 2-8 Visual Recognition: Seconds			
	Tape 2-6 Tonal Memory			
	Tape 2-7 Imitation with Notation: Seconds			
	Conference: Intonation			
	Ex. 2-9 Intonation: Seconds			
	Tape 2-8 Anticipation: Seconds			
	Tape 2-9 Aural Recognition: Seconds			
	Conference: Composing Interval Drills			
	Tape 2-10 Error Correction: Intervals			
	Conference: Rehearsed Melodies			
	REHEARSED MELODIES			
	SIGHT-READING			
	MORE DIFFICULT			
	Conference: Dictation			

Page		Completed	Answers	Comments
	DICTATION			
	Tape 2-11 Intervals			
	Tape 2-12 Melody			
	UNIT 3			
	INTERVALS			
	Thirds—Major and Minor			
	Tape 3-1 Listening: Thirds			
	Ex. 3-1 Visual Recognition of Intervals			
	Ex. 3-2 Intonation: Thirds			
	Tape 3-2 Tonal Memory			
	Tape 3-3 Imitation with Notation: Thirds			
	Conference: Fusing			
	Tape 3-4 Fusing: Thirds			
	Conference: Learning Intervals			
	Tape 3-5 Anticipation: Thirds			
	Tape 3-6 Aural Recognition: Thirds			
	Tape 3-7 Error Correction: Melody			
	Conference: RP and Intervallic Illusions			
	Tape 3-8 Aural Recognition: Review of Intervals			
	MAJOR SCALES			
	MINOR SCALES			
	Ex. 3-3 Intonation: Minor Scales			
	Dynamics			
	REHEARSED RHYTHM			
	REHEARSED MELODIES			
	Conference: Ensembles			
	ENSEMBLES			
	SIGHT-READING			
	MORE DIFFICULT			
	DICTATION			
	Tape 3-9 Rhythm, Melodic Motives, Melody			

Page	UNIT 4	Com-pleted	An-swers	Comments
	RHYTHM			
	Level 4 (Simple Subdivision)			
	Ex. 4-1 Note Values			
	REHEARSED RHYTHM			
	Level 4: Ratios			
	Ex. 4-2 Note Values			
	Tape 4-1 Imitation with Notation: Rhythm			
	Tape 4-2 Error Correction: Rhythm			
	Conference: Practicing Rhythm			
	Ex. 4-3 Rehearsed Rhythm			
	INTERVALS			
	Perfect Fourth			
	Tape 4-3 Listening: Perfect Fourth			
	Tape 4-4 Tonal Memory			
	Ex. 4-4 Visual Recognition of Intervals			
	Ex. 4-5 Intonation: Perfect Fourth			
	Tape 4-5 Imitation with Notation: Intervals			
	Tape 4-6 Anticipation: Intervals			
	Tape 4-7 Fusing: Perfect Fourth			
	Tape 4-8 Aural Recognition: Intervals			
	Tape 4-9 Error Correction: Intervals			
	Tape 4-10 Error Correction: Melody			
	The C Clef			
	Ex. 4-6 Alto Clef			
	Ex. 4-7 Scanning			
	REHEARSED MELODIES			
	Conference: Performing Ensembles			
	ENSEMBLES			
	SIGHT-READING			
	MORE DIFFICULT			
	DICTATION			
	Tape 4-11 Rhythm, Motives			
	Tape 4-12 Melody			

Page	UNIT 5	Com-pleted	An-swers	Comments
	RHYTHM			
	Level 3 Compound Meters			
	Ex. 5-1 Meter Signatures			
	Level 3 Rhythms			
	Ex. 5-2 Rehearsed Rhythm			
	Ex. 5-3 Meter Signatures			
	Ex. 5-4 Note Values			
	Tape 5-1 Anticipation: Rhythm			
	Tape 5-2 Error Correction: Rhythm			
	Ex. 5-5 Rehearsed Rhythm			
	INTERVALS			
	Perfect Fifth			
	Tape 5-3 Listening: Perfect Fifth			
	Tape 5-4 Tonal Memory			
	Ex. 5-6 Visual Recognition			
	Ex. 5-7 Intonation: Perfect Fifth			
	Tape 5-5 Imitation with Notation: Intervals, Review of Intervals			
	Tape 5-6 Anticipation: Intervals			
	Tape 5-7 Fusing: Perfect Fifth, Review of Intervals			
	Tape 5-8 Aural Recognition: Intervals			
	Tape 5-9 Error Correction: Melody			
	HARMONY			
	Triads			
	Ex. 5-8 Visual Recognition of Triads			
	Ex. 5-9 Fusing: Major and Minor Triads			
	Ex. 5-10 Fusing: Triads			
	Ex. 5-11 Major and Minor Triads			
	Tape 5-10 Aural Recognition: Triads			
	Tape 5-11 Error Correction: Triads			
	Two-Part Music—Parallel, Similar, Oblique, and Contrary Motion			
	Tape 5-12 Listening: Two-Part Music			
	Tape 5-13 Aural Recognition: Two-Part Music			

Page		Com-pleted	An-swers	Comments
	Conference: Two-Part Music			
	Tape 5-14 Error Correction: Two-Part Music			
	Ex. 5-12 Tenor Clef			
	Ex. 5-13 Scanning			
	REHEARSED MELODIES			
	ENSEMBLES			
	SIGHT-READING			
	MORE DIFFICULT			
	DICTATION			
	Tape 5-15 Rhythm			
	Tape 5-16 Motives, Melody			
	Tape 5-17 Two-Part Music			
	UNIT 6			
	INTERVALS			
	Sixths—Major and Minor			
	Tape 6-1 Listening: Sixths			
	Ex. 6-1 Visual Recognition: Sixths			
	Tape 6-2 Tonal Memory			
	Tape 6-3 Imitation with Notation: Sixths			
	Ex. 6-2 Intonation: Sixths			
	Conference: Timbre and Interval Recognition			
	Tape 6-4 Anticipation: Sixths, Review of Intervals			
	Tape 6-5 Fusing, Review of Intervals			
	Tape 6-6 Aural Recognition: Review of Intervals			
	Tape 6-7 Error Correction: Melody			
	HARMONY			
	Tape 6-8 Anticipation: Major and Minor Triads			
	Tape 6-9 Function			
	Function			
	Ex. 6-3 Fusing: Tonic and Dominant			
	Ex. 6-4 Anticipation: Review of Major and Minor Triads			
	Tape 6-10 Anticipation: Tonic and Dominant Spacing			

318

Page		Completed	Answers	Comments
	Ex. 6-5 Spacing: Harmony			
	Tape 6-11 Listening: Harmony			
	Tape 6-12 Aural Recognition: Harmony			
	Ex. 6-6 Harmonizing Folksongs			
	Ex. 6-7 Fusing: Two-Part Music Accents			
	RHYTHM			
	Meter Changes			
	Ex. 6-8 Rehearsed Rhythm: Accents and Meter Changes			
	Ex. 6-9 Scanning			
	REHEARSED MELODIES			
	ENSEMBLES			
	SIGHT-READING			
	MORE DIFFICULT			
	DICTATION			
	Tape 6-13 Rhythm			
	Tape 6-14 Motives, Melody			
	Tape 6-15 Two-Part Music			
	Tape 6-16 Harmony			
	UNIT 7			
	INTERVALS			
	Sevenths—Major and Minor			
	Ex. 7-1 Visual Recognition and Review of Intervals			
	Tape 7-1 Listening: Sevenths			
	Tape 7-2 Tonal Memory			
	Tape 7-3 Imitation with Notation			
	Ex. 7-2 Intonation			
	Tape 7-4 Anticipation: Sevenths			
	Tape 7-5 Anticipation: Review of Intervals			
	Tape 7-6 Fusing			
	Tape 7-7 Aural Recognition: Sevenths, Review of Intervals			
	Tape 7-8 Error Correction: Intervals			

Page		Completed	Answers	Comments
	Tape 7-9 Error Correction: Melody			
	HARMONY			
	Subdominant Function			
	Tape 7-10 Listening: Harmony—Subdominant			
	Conference: Fusing Parts			
	Ex. 7-3 Fusing: Function of Major and Minor Triads			
	Soprano Factors			
	Tape 7-11 Listening: Factors			
	Tape 7-12 Listening: Harmony—Subdominant			
	Conference: Polyphony			
	RHYTHM			
	Ex. 7-4 Scanning			
	REHEARSED RHYTHM			
	REHEARSED MELODIES			
	ENSEMBLES			
	SIGHT-READING			
	MORE DIFFICULT			
	Tape 7-13 Error Correction: Two-Part Music			
	DICTATION			
	Tape 7-14 Rhythm, Melody			
	Conference: Two-Part Music			
	Tape 7-15 Two-Part Music			
	Tape 7-16 Harmony			
	UNIT 8			
	INTERVALS			
	Tritone			
	Tape 8-1 Listening: Tritone			
	Tape 8-2 Tonal Memory			
	Tape 8-3 Imitation with Notation: Tritone			
	Ex. 8-1 Visual Recognition: Intervals			
	Ex. 8-2 Intonation: Tritone			
	Tape 8-4 Anticipation: Tritone			

Page		Completed	Answers	Comments
	Tape 8-5 Fusing: Tritone, Review of Intervals			
	Tape 8-6 Aural Recognition: Review of Intervals			
	Tape 8-7 Error Correction: Review of Intervals			
	Octave			
	Tape 8-8 Tonal Memory			
	Ex. 8-3 Visual Recognition: Intervals			
	Ex. 8-4 Intonation: Octave			
	Tape 8-9 Imitation with Notation: Review of Intervals			
	Tape 8-10 Anticipation: Review of Intervals			
	Conference: Practice Schedule			
	Tape 8-11 Fusing, Review of Intervals			
	Conference: Interval Categories			
	Tape 8-12 Aural Recognition: Intervals			
	Tape 8-13 Error Correction: Review of Intervals			
	Conference: More than one RP			
	HARMONY			
	Dominant Seventh Chord			
	Ex. 8-5 Fusing: Dominant Seventh Chord			
	Ex. 8-6 Listening: Dominant Seventh Chord			
	Tape 8-14 Aural Recognition: Chords			
	Tape 8-15 Aural Recognition: Review of Chords			
	Tape 8-16 Aural Recognition: Harmony—Dominant Seventh Chord			
	Ex. 8-7 Listening: Harmony			
	Tape 8-17 Error Correction: Two-Part Music			
	Ex. 8-8 Scanning			
	REHEARSED RHYTHM			
	REHEARSED MELODIES			
	ENSEMBLES			
	SIGHT-READING			
	DICTATION			

Page		Completed	Answers	Comments
	Tape 8-18 Rhythm, Melody			
	Tape 8-19 Two-Part Music			
	Tape 8-20 Harmony			
	UNIT 9			
	RHYTHM			
	Level 6			
	Ex. 9-1 Notation: Rhythm			
	Ex.9-2 Rhythm: Ratios			
	Tape 9-1 Imitation with Notation: Rhythm—Level 6			
	Tape 9-2 Error Correction: Rhythm—Level 6			
	INTERVALS			
	Tape 9-3 Tonal Memory: Review of Intervals			
	Ex. 9-3 Visual Recognition: Review of Intervals			
	Ex. 9-4 Intonation: Multiple RPs			
	Conference: Inversion of Intervals			
	Tape 9-4 Imitation with Notation: Review of Intervals			
	Tape 9-5 Anticipation: Review of Intervals			
	Tape 9-6 Aural Recognition: Review of Intervals			
	Tape 9-7 Error Correction: Melody			
	Ex. 9-5 Fusing: I, IV, and V Chords			
	HARMONY			
	First Inversion of Chords			
	Tape 9-8 Listening: Triads in Root Position and First Inversion			
	Tape 9-9 Aural Recognition: Triads in Root Position and First Inversion			
	Tape 9-10 Listening: Harmony—First Inversion			
	Tape 9-11 Anticipation: Harmony			
	Tape 9-12 Error Correction: Harmony			
	Tape 9-13 Aural Recognition: Two-Part Music			
	Tape 9-14 Error Correction: Two-Part Music			

Page		Completed	Answers	Comments
	Ex. 9-6 Scanning			
	REHEARSED MELODIES			
	ENSEMBLES			
	SIGHT-READING			
	MORE DIFFICULT			
	DICTATION			
	Tape 9-15 Rhythm, Melody			
	Tape 9-16 Two-Part Music			
	Tape 9-17 Harmony			
	UNIT 10			
	INTERVALS			
	Harmonic Minor Scale			
	Tape 10-1 Tonal Memory			
	Ex. 10-1 Visual Recognition: Augmented Second			
	Ex. 10-2 Intonation: Harmonic Minor Scale			
	Tape 10-2 Imitation with Notation: Review of Intervals			
	Tape 10-3 Imitation with Notation: Inversion of Intervals			
	Tape 10-4 Anticipation: Review of Intervals			
	Tape 10-5 Aural Recognition: Review of Intervals			
	Tape 10-6 Error Correction: Melody			
	HARMONY			
	First Inversion of the Dominant Seventh Chord			
	Tape 10-7 Listening with Notation: V_5^6			
	Ex. 10-3 Fusing: V_5^6			
	Tape 10-8 Aural Recognition: Harmony			
	vii° Chord			
	Tape 10-9 Listening with Notation: vii° Triad			
	Ex. 10-4 Fusing: Diminished Triad			
	Tape 10-10 Aural Recognition: Harmony			
	Ex. 10-5 Fusing			

Page		Completed	Answers	Comments
	Ex. 10-6 Visual Recognition: Chords			
	Ex. 10-7 Fusing: Function			
	Tape 10-11 Anticipation: Harmony			
	Tape 10-12 Error Correction: Harmony			
	Tape 10-13 Error Correction: Two-Part Music			
	Ex. 10-8 Scanning			
	REHEARSED RHYTHM			
	REHEARSED MELODIES			
	ENSEMBLES			
	SIGHT-READING			
	MORE DIFFICULT			
	DICTATION			
	Tape 10-14 Rhythm, Melody			
	Tape 10-15 Two-Part Music			
	Tape 10-16 Harmony			
	Tape 10-17 Harmony			
	UNIT 11			
	RHYTHM			
	Level 8			
	Ex. 11-1 Rhythm: Level 8			
	Tape 11-1 Error Correction: Rhythm			
	MODES			
	Mixolydian			
	Tape 11-2 Listening: Mixolydian			
	Conference: Tonal Memory			
	Ex. 11-2 Intonation: Mixolydian Mode, Review			
	Ex. 11-3 Visual Recognition: Mixolydian Mode			
	Tape 11-3 Tonal Memory			
	INTERVALS			
	Ex. 11-4 Inversion of Intervals			
	Ex. 11-5 Mirror Inversion of Intervals			
	Tape 11-4 Anticipation: Review of Intervals			
	Tape 11-5 Error Correction: Review of Intervals			
	Tape 11-6 Error Correction: Melody			

Page		Com-pleted	An-swers	Comments
	Tape 11-7 Error Correction: Two-Part Music			
	HARMONY			
	Second Inversion of the Triad			
	Tape 11-8 Listening with Notation: Second Inversion of the Triad			
	Ex. 11-6 Fusing: Second Inversion of the Triad			
	Second Inversion of the Dominant Seventh Chord			
	Tape 11-9 Listening with Notation: V_3^4			
	Ex. 11-7 Fusing: Second Inversion of the Dominant Seventh Chord			
	Ex. 11-8 Fusing: Function			
	Tape 11-10 Aural Recognition: Chords			
	Ex. 11-9 Visual Recognition: Chords			
	Tape 11-11 Anticipation: Harmony			
	Tape 11-12 Error Correction: Harmony			
	Fermata			
	Ex. 11-10 Scanning			
	REHEARSED MELODIES			
	ENSEMBLES			
	SIGHT-READING			
	MORE DIFFICULT			
	DICTATION			
	Tape 11-13 Rhythm, Melody			
	Tape 11-14 Two-Part Music			
	Tape 11-15 Harmony			
	Tape 11-16 Harmony			
	UNIT 12			
	HARMONY			
	Third Inversion of the Dominant Seventh Chord			
	Tape 12-1 Listening with Notation: V_2^4			
	Ex. 12-1 Fusing: V_2^4			
	Ex. 12-2 Fusing: Function			
	Tape 12-2 Aural Recognition: Review of Chords			

Page		Completed	Answers	Comments
	Ex. 12-3 Visual Recognition of Chords			
	Tape 12-3 Anticipation: Harmony			
	Tape 12-4 Error Correction: Harmony			
	Conference: Review of Listening Experiences in Harmony			
	MODES			
	Dorian Mode			
	Tape 12-5 Dorian Mode			
	Tape 12-6 Tonal Memory			
	Conference: Intonation Studies			
	Ex. 12-4 Intonation: Dorian Mode			
	Ex. 12-5 Mirror Inversion of Motives			
	Ionian and Aeolian Modes			
	INTERVALS			
	Tape 12-7 Anticipation: Review of Intervals and Inversions			
	Tape 12-8 Error Correction: Intervals			
	Tape 12-9 Error Correction: Melody			
	Tape 12-10 Error Correction: Two-Part Music			
	RHYTHM			
	Mixed Levels			
	Ex. 12-6 Rehearsed Rhythm			
	Tape 12-11 Error Correction: Rhythm			
	Tempo Changes			
	Ex. 12-7 Tempo Changes			
	Ex. 12-8 Rehearsed Rhythm			
	Ex. 12-9 Scanning			
	REHEARSED MELODIES			
	ENSEMBLES			
	SIGHT-READING			
	MORE DIFFICULT			
	DICTATION			
	Tape 12-12 Rhythm, Melody			
	Tape 12-13 Two-Part Music			
	Conference: Modal Harmony			

Page		Completed	Answer	Comments
	Tape 12-14 Harmony			
	Tape 12-15 Harmony			
	UNIT 13			
	MODES			
	Phrygian Mode			
	Tape 13-1 Listening			
	Tape 13-2 Tonal Memory			
	Ex. 13-1 Intonation: Phrygian Mode			
	Ex. 13-2 Mirror Inversion			
	INTERVALS			
	Tape 13-3 Anticipation: Review of Intervals			
	Tape 13-4 Error Correction: Intervals			
	Tape 13-5 Error Correction: Melody			
	Conference: Multiple RPs			
	Chart of Scales and Chords			
	HARMONY			
	Secondary Triads			
	Conference: Listening Goals			
	Tape 13-6 Listening with Notation: vi Chord			
	Ex. 13-3 Fusing: Function			
	Tape 13-7 Aural Recognition: Review of Chords			
	Ex. 13-4 Visual Recognition: Chords			
	Tape 13-8 Anticipation: Harmony			
	Tape 13-9 Fusing: Harmony			
	Tape 13-10 Error Correction: Harmony			
	Tape 13-11 Error Correction: Two-Part Music			
	RHYTHM			
	Mixed Basic Durations			
	Conference: Comparison of Mixed Levels and Mixed BDs			
	Ex. 13-5 Mixed BDs			
	Ex. 13-6 Mixed BDs or Mixed Levels			
	Tape 13-12 Error Correction: Rhythm			
	Ex. 13-7 Scanning			

Page		Completed	Answers	Comments
	REHEARSED MELODIES			
	ENSEMBLES			
	SIGHT-READING			
	MORE DIFFICULT			
	DICTATION			
	Tape 13-13 Rhythm, Melody			
	Tape 13-14 Two-Part Music			
	Tape 13-15 Harmony			
	Tape 13-16 Harmony			
	UNIT 14			
	HARMONY			
	ii Chord			
	Tape 14-1 Listening with Notation: ii Chord			
	Ex. 14-1 Fusing: Harmony—ii Chord			
	Tape 14-2 Aural Recognition: Review of Chords			
	Ex. 14-2 Visual Recognition: Chords			
	Tape 14-3 Anticipation: Harmony			
	Tape 14-4 Fusing: Harmony			
	Tape 14-5 Error Correction: Harmony			
	Tape 14-6 Error Correction: Two-Part Music			
	MODES			
	Lydian Mode			
	Tape 14-7 Listening: Lydian Mode			
	Tape 14-8 Tonal Memory			
	Ex. 14-3 Intonation: Lydian Mode			
	Conference: Similarities and Differences in Modes			
	INTERVALS			
	Tape 14-9 Anticipation: Review of Intervals			
	Tape 14-10 Error Correction: Intervals			
	Tape 14-11 Error Correction: Rhythm			
	Tape 14-12 Error Correction: Melody			
	REHEARSED RHYTHM			
	REHEARSED MELODIES			
	ENSEMBLES			

Page		Com-pleted	An-swer	Comments
	SIGHT-READING			
	MORE DIFFICULT			
	DICTATION			
	Tape 14-13 Rhythm, Melody			
	Tape 14-14 Two-Part Music			
	Tape 14-15 Harmony			
	Tape 14-16 Harmony			
	UNIT 15			
	PENTATONIC SCALES			
	Ex. 15-1 Singing Pentatonic Scales			
	Ex. 15-2 Visual Recognition: Scales			
	Tape 15-1 Tonal Memory			
	Ex. 15-3 Intonation: Pentatonic Scale			
	INTERVALS			
	Tape 15-2 Anticipation: Review of Intervals			
	Tape 15-3 Error Correction: Intervals			
	Tape 15-4 Error Correction: Melody			
	Ex. 15-4 Intonation: Modes			
	Tape 15-5 Aural Recognition: Modes			
	HARMONY			
	iii Chord			
	Tape 15-6 Listening with Notation: iii Chord			
	Ex. 15-5 Fusing: Function—iii Chord			
	Tape 15-7 Aural Recognition: Review of Chords			
	Ex. 15-6 Visual Recognition: Chords			
	Tape 15-8 Anticipation: Harmony			
	Tape 15-9 Fusing: Harmony			
	Tape 15-10 Error Correction: Harmony			
	Tape 15-11 Error Correction: Two-Part Music			
	RHYTHM			
	Tape 15-12 Error Correction: Rhythm			
	Ex. 15-7 Scanning			
	REHEARSED RHYTHM			
	REHEARSED MELODIES			

Page		Completed	Answers	Comments
	ENSEMBLES			
	SIGHT-READING			
	MORE DIFFICULT			
	DICTATION			
	Tape 15-13 Rhythm, Melody			
	Tape 15-14 Two-Part Music			
	Tape 15-15 Harmony			
	Tape 15-16 Harmony			